In the midst of plenty

Poverty in the midst of plenty is a paradox that must not go unchallenged in this country. Ours is the wealthiest of nations, yet one-sixth of our people live below minimal levels of health, housing, food and education—in the slums of cities, in migratory labor camps, in economically depressed areas, on Indian reservations. In addition, special hardships are faced by our senior citizens, dependent children, and the victims of mental illness, mental retardation and other disabling misfortunes.

President JOHN F. KENNEDY in a letter dated April 10, 1963, to Lyndon B. Johnson, President of the United States Senate

In the Midst of Plenty

The Poor in America

Ben H. Bagdikian

BEACON PRESS   BOSTON

ACKNOWLEDGMENTS

My first thanks go to the many people who permitted me to enter their homes and, briefly, their lives and who talked frankly and deeply about their past, their problems, and their hopes for the future. Not all of them are described in this book and those who are do not always appear under their true names. But from each I learned something.

I am grateful to *The Saturday Evening Post*, for which I first did research on this subject. Much of the material in this book came from that project and some is from the article I wrote for the *Post*, "The Invisible Americans."

Wherever I went—private homes, labor unions, welfare agencies, Indian Reservation, Skid Row, government office—I found men and women ready to help, so many I cannot thank them all by name.

Any flaws in the book are mine.

B.H.B.

Washington, D.C.
September 14, 1963

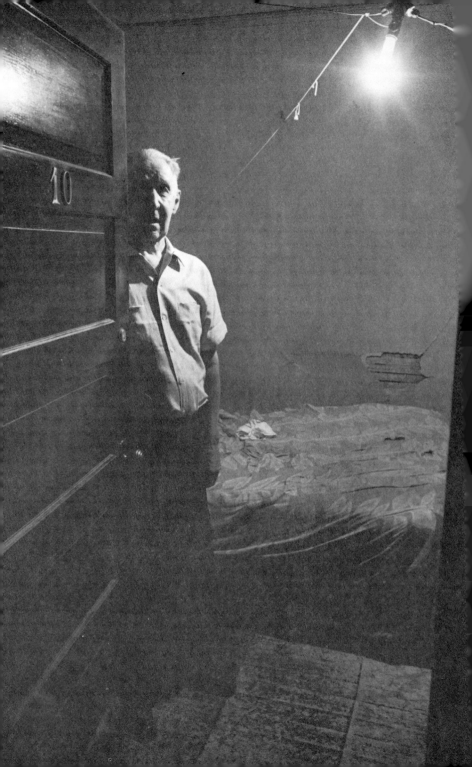

CONTENTS

CHAPTER ONE

Out of sight, out of mind ...

There in the shade of the hamburger stand was the guitar player—dark glasses, tin cup, strumming loosely, singing loudly—the popular image of the remaining poor in America: the exceptional unfortunate one, the irreducible special case. He was scarcely noticeable in the surrounding crowds who wandered into five-and-tens and department stores on their consuming rounds.

The scene framed by the window of my rented car was in downtown Columbia, South Carolina, but it could have been in a thousand American cities. To the motorized middle-class American eye, the poor hardly exist.

The thought had occurred to me an hour earlier as the plane lowered over the lovely spring countryside. Where on the landscape below were the signs of poverty? Not on the big concrete highway where the cars and their slanting afternoon shadows raced past new shopping centers and geometric clusters of painted cottages. But if the eye left the main valley to go up a side road to a smaller valley, to still another dirt road that splayed out on a sudden uptilt of eroded land, there they were: the collapsing shacks, the tilting privies, the rotting farm buildings with smoke curling out of a roofpipe, hidden from the eye of the automobilized citizen, out of sight and

1

out of mind, the ill-fed and ill-housed forgotten fifth of America.

The impoverished are forgotten because, among other reasons, the automobile and the airplane are new wombs for personal withdrawal, private capsules that impel their passengers along predetermined paths of affluence.

As I drove the car through downtown Columbia I knew very well that somewhere behind the big buildings were the row houses of the urban Negro poor. But I was curious to test on the ground what I had seen from the air. I drove by graceful homes aglow with azalea, through the outskirts with their Dairy Queens and root beer stands, until there was only field and forest. Then I took the first side road I could find, then another, each time choosing the smaller of every fork until I turned into one lane just wide enough for the car and had to stop short.

When the dust settled, the chromium-plated car dominated a tiny scene. On one side was a weary garden hemmed in by rusted hoops of wire, some tired white iris still nodding from the rush of the car. On the other side was a tin-roofed cottage, tipped slightly as it rested on loose brick piles. From under a worn front stoop came two ambivalent mongrels, unsure whether they were frightened or frightening. Out of the door came a tall, scrawny Negro woman. The porch boards gave a little under her step. She had grey kinky hair, her upper teeth were mostly eroded away, and she looked me straight in the eye. Driving at random, guided only by the impulse to get off the beaten path, I met Rebecca Franklin. It was, it so happened, her birthday.

Inside the living room of the five-room shack the younger children giggled in from the kitchen. To make excuses to see the visitor they brought in empty paper bags and folded towels as gifts to tease their mother. *"Happy birthday, Mama."* After a time this irritated her. She looked steadily at the children and then sighed in resignation. *"I'm 48,"* she said. *"I know I look older."*

Her husband died from injuries in an automobile accident six years ago and left her with twelve children, ages six to twenty-seven. The youngest eight are still at home. Because she is a widow with dependent children whose husband was under Social Security she gets $70 a month in Federal survivors insurance. She earns about $100 a month cleaning and cooking for white families in town. Her older married children outside the state send her about $100 in cash a year. For a family of nine, $2200 a year is poverty.

Because she cooks for others, Mrs. Franklin assumes that her own food costs nothing. She spends $30 a week for the children's food, or 70 per cent of her income. At times she has enough for the 25 cents a day the children need for a hot lunch at their school but usually they are limited to 3 cents a day for milk. If there have been "extra" expenses during the month, on the last few days before the check they eat only bread, salt pork and cane syrup. The children have never been to a doctor or a dentist. They have no television set. In the evening they cut wood for the kitchen stove and if, after that and homework there is still time, they go to a neighbor's house to watch some TV. There is no running water in the house, but there is a *World Book Encyclopedia*, its payments made by a daughter in Connecticut, and there is an electric refrigerator, its payments made by a son in Philadelphia.

Mrs. Franklin may be eligible for welfare aid but she doesn't get it. "*After my husband's insurance gave out I went down and applied. I answered all their questions and then got a letter saying I hadn't proved to them I needed welfare. I told them everything they asked. I'm not going to lie for welfare. I'm not going to take a white person to speak for me. So I decided to work and take a chance the children would be all right while I'm out.*"

She held her head stiffly. "*Well, all my grown children but one finished high school, and that one quit after the eleventh grade because he had to go to a sanitarium with the TB. And the younger ones will finish, too. My tenth grade girl needs a pair of shoes right now if she's going to finish school this year. I got a dollar for my birthday from my pastor, and $2 from the lady I work for, and $5 my older children sent me by mail. So my girl will get to finish tenth grade; I'll get her a pair of tennis shoes.*"

She pursed her lips and straightened a magazine on the living room table.

"*Here it's almost the end of the school year but already it seems like the awful months.*"

The awful months?

"*Yes. The awful months. August. December. March. August you got to find clothes if the kids are going to school that year. December you just have to find some money somehow for Christmas presents. March is usually Easter and everyone else will have new clothes and you've got to try to find some little thing bright and new so the kids won't be ashamed to go to church or to school.*"

There is more to Rebecca Franklin's story, but though she is better off than most in spirit and in strength she is a reflection of the majority of the American poor, engaged in the desperate struggle to maintain the framework of civilized life against the crush of brute survival. For the country at large there are wry jokes about Christmas bills and standard complaints about school clothes, but after this ritual is completed there is no question that school is taken for granted as the required gate to opportunity, and that the Christmas and Easter seasons are times for renewal and joy. These are real for most of the poor but for them they are also terrible reminders that the symbols of civilized life are fading away and their families are losing their foothold on normal American culture. They become "the awful months."

In Rebecca Franklin's tilting home were the standard elements of life among the poor: the awful months, the pinch of real hunger at month's end, the regular economic catastrophe of disintegrated shoes, the absence of medical care, and in the countryside the universal leaky roof.

But the worst ghost of all is loneliness and isolation. There are curtains that separate the poor from their countrymen, symbolized by the hills that shield the valleys of misery, and the dirt roads that discourage fast-moving cars, and the ugly decrepitude that keeps respectable people out of the slums. But these are physical manifestations. The real isolation of the poor is from the warmth and hope of ordinary life. This is a paradox in a rich and compassionate country. It should not be economically difficult to give meaning to the lives of the 6 out of every 100 workers who are unemployed, nor for the 94 to reach out in human help to the 6. But this does not happen in any effective way, not because Americans are cruel but because they are looking the other way. The poor have drifted out of the national consciousness. Had I stayed on the big highways and the busiest streets I would have missed most of the poor.

This book will try to describe what it means to live on the other side of the curtain, to endure day by day the lonesome life of the poor. It has been impossible to enter the lives of the poor without realizing how close they are to salvation. They are not, most of them, without spirit and hope, yet they are not confronted with the normal handholds with which the non-poor pull themselves to self-sufficiency. They do not, initially, shun normal society, yet normal society stares through them unseeing. They do not shrink from probing for a way out, but for the poor there are nothing but stone walls. We have yet to learn, in the 1960's, something America has shown in abundance in the past: how to reach the poor economically, socially, educationally, and with simple humanity.

One reason we have failed is that we are not yet convinced that there is truly a world inside our society in which the American dream is dying, where when it rains at night everyone gets up to move beds away from the leaks. Where there is no electricity but discarded refrigerators are valued to keep food safe from rats. Where regularly in the last week of the month whole families live on things like berries and bread. Where children in winter sleep on floors in burlap bags and their lung X-rays at age twelve look like old men's. Where students drift hungry and apathetic through school and their parents die ten or twenty or thirty years earlier than their countrymen.

We are inclined to think that this happens only to the physical and psychological cripples, that they suffer in small numbers in isolated geographic pockets. But the poor are everywhere. There are at least 20,000,000 in the United States and, depending on how hungry and unhealthy you call "poor," perhaps as many as 54,000,000. Every city and every region has them and in a few unfortunate places there is scarcely anyone else.

For the most part these men, women, and children are not made so differently from their fellow Americans. But they have had the bad luck to be born in a poor region, or in a dying or automating industry, or on a small farm. They may have a dark skin color. They may be sick. Or they may have lost their jobs after they were forty years old—too old to find a new steady job but not old enough to die. Or, like the American Indian and the small farmer, they may merely be born into an obsolete culture.

The poor in the 1960's are largely invisible. They are obscured by The National Average. Since World War II it has been taken for granted that the United States, with the world's highest standard of living, has eliminated poverty. For 80 per cent of the population this is true and this 80 per cent understandably assume it is the same for all. The poor are also hidden by the new city where more than ever before the most wretched people are unseen in the central cores while their comfortable compatriots are gone to the suburbs. And the poor are concealed by modern apparel: all Americans tend to dress casually and modern dyes keep old clothes unfaded.

But poverty is not gone. It is still here, for different reasons than in the past, some of these reasons deeply disturbing.

The American poor are incomparably more lucky than those in Asia and Africa and the Middle East who die by the hundreds in the streets. The American poor live better than the average citizen in many an underdeveloped country. They are better off in important ways than the rich of a hundred years ago and royalty of the Dark Ages.

But poverty is not measured by history. It is measured by the standards of a man's own community. If most of America is well-fed, the man who can't find three meals a day for his family is poor. If most of America has modern weather-proof housing, the man whose home is leaky and has no piped water is poor. If most of America has enough medical care to stay alive until age seventy, the man who can't afford to live beyond age fifty-five is poor. Such a man is poor statistically. But he is poor in a more damaging way: he is a failure in his neighbor's eye and in his own.

Most of the poor are caught in a vast convulsion in the human landscape of the United States, a change that reflects brilliant prosperity with deep shadows of persisting poverty. Farms are becoming great mechanized operations, surviving through science, size and big investment. In the process country people are being squeezed off the land— more than a million a year—and are fleeing to the cities.

Yet, the cities are having their troubles. The traditional urban foothold for the novice from the country, the unskilled factory or construction job, is being eliminated by automation. The usual clues to successful city living, the visible example of friendly—or even unfriendly—neighbors, are gone as city folk abandon neighborhoods en masse or move to the suburbs. The newcomers are left to wander the asphalt jungles with only similarly bewildered people to look at, while their children attend schools filled exclusively with overwhelmed students like themselves.

Nevertheless, the city has much excitement. It has some jobs. And it has a tradition that the starving shall be fed. The tide continues toward metropolis. At this moment millions of rural Americans are merely waiting for a free ride, or the bus fare, or the hint of a job, or the last vestige of family loyalty to die so that they can flee the rural misery they know for the risk of urban misery unknown.

CHAPTER TWO

"Children Are Not to Run, Shout, or Play"

Into the cities they pour, refugees from a silent revolution.

In Chicago the white folk from the countryside come mostly by Trailway bus, carrying all they own: a suitcase tied with rope, an old trunk, three shopping bags, a folded baby buggy, a bag of grits, clutching a letter from a relative come earlier with an address and a warning, "Don't take the cabs, they'll cheat you."

If they are colored they come mostly by that great iron artery in Southern Negro life, the Illinois Central Railroad, getting off in awe under the largest building they ever saw, carrying their old suitcases and trunks, cardboard boxes with clothes and pans, and they, too, have a carefully written address, an address that may no longer exist because newcomers go to the slums and massive redevelopment is turning many slums into vacant lots or luxury apartments.

If they are American Indians they may come in rickety old cars from the Dakotas and Utah and Arizona, fleeing the hunger of the reservations, making Chicago the fourth largest concentration of aborigines in the United States.

They all gravitate toward the city, entering Chicago at the rate of fifty a day.

In a city as big as Chicago the newcomers face a

10

strange new world. Old courage is not enough, previous skills meaningless, and what may have been minor disadvantages in education or family cohesion suddenly become catastrophic. It is possible, walking among the newcomers in their tenements, to hear these stories and these voices, and to see these signs:

"Why, this contract you signed says you have to pay carrying charges for the furniture that are more than the furniture itself! Didn't you read this before you signed it?"

"Well, Sister, the man said it would be a small charge and I couldn't find my glasses that day."

"You mean you can't read, don't you?"

"Well, not very well, Sister."

The twenty-four-year-old white girl, infant in arms, herding two other small children before her, has hitchhiked continuously for two days and two nights from West Virginia and found her husband in the middle of Chicago during a blizzard, but when a social worker gives her applications to fill out and bus tokens to get to the agency for help, the girl who has braved four hundred miles of the unknown, telephones five times in panic because the buses, the city, and the forms in triplicate are frightening.

"Mr. Donovan, my husband's back from jail so the welfare cut out my ADC because I got a unreported male in the house. Does that mean my kids can't eat because their Daddy's home?"

At Stewart Elementary School in Chicago about one thousand students enter in the fall and about one thousand students leave before June because their parents have been evicted, have departed the district for another house, or have gone back South. A teacher said, "It's hard to teach a child much of anything in a school with a 100 per cent turnover every year."

"Joe, you got to stay and help me. I need help."

"Ma, I'm going. I'm leaving for good. I don't know what I'll do but I can't stand it no more. I'm seventeen and I'll get along somehow. It's not my fault Pa's a drunk and you got eleven kids. Now you'll only have ten."

The heavy black pencilled letters, written large and painfully, are on grey cardboard tacked to the plaster in the damp corridor of 4860 North Winthrop: "Absolutely Do Not Throw Trash Out Bathroom Windows. Children Are Not to Run, Shout, or Play in Halls."

But it is not just Chicago. It is the same in New York, Los Angeles, Philadelphia, Detroit, Cleveland, Washington, St. Louis—all the great cities. In the last four decades a vast migration of 27,000,000 men, women, and children have flocked to metropolis. It is greater than the international migration which at its fullest flow from 1880 to 1920 brought 24,000,000 foreigners to America's cities. This time it is native Americans.

Almost all of them are poor. An alarming number of them remain poor for a long time.

The poverty of the newcomers is familiar and at the same time different. Prolonged lack of money can arise from a number of causes but whatever its cause it can have serious side effects that deepen the disease.

There are enormous differences in each person's response to adversity and because some people have been celebrated for personal triumph over poverty this has led to the assumption—usually by the well-fed—that to be poor makes one more noble. This was never true for most of the poor and it is not true now. Yet the belief persists that the poor compared with the affluent ought to be more honest, more resourceful, more puritanical, more disciplined, more resilient against despair, more emotionally stable, and simultaneously more aggressive and more submissive. They are not. Poverty is the pressure of living at the bottom of the social sea and this pressure finds the weakness in every personality. Poverty is dirty, vermin-infested, cold in winter, broiling in summer, and worst of all it is lonely and self-reproaching.

Ironically, the native American poor of the 1960's are worse off in some ways than the foreign immigrants of two generations ago. Both came practically penniless, went into the worst housing, got the worst jobs, and suffered the isolation and discrimination that comes to the impoverished stranger.

But the foreigners had their own culture and countrymen and history to give them assurance while they were being shunned by the new culture. In the old days if a man was disdained as a "wop" or a "mick" or a "kike" he or his parents knew that there were a time and a place in which the Italians ruled the world and created a great culture, or the Irish wrenched freedom from the world's greatest power and defended their Roman Catholic faith, or the Jews shared the making of modern civilization and survived the suffering millennia with learning and art. The lash of prejudice made its scars, as it always does, but there was some psychological solace in one's own history and bitter satisfaction that the tormentor was so ignorant he didn't even know this history. But the Negro called "nigger" or turned away with a crocodilian "Sir," and the Alabama white sneeringly called "hillbilly" hear this from their own countrymen. From the viper within the nest there is little room for retreat.

The foreign immigrant had his small solace but he also had a spur to drive him on. His was a total commitment to the new land: he had no way to leave. He could not hitchhike back to the farm, or take a bus to the home village, or go back again to the stream of migrant agricultural workers. Most had barely managed the ocean voyage here. There was no turning back.

They came from abroad at an opportune time. The New World was abuilding—railroads, canals, factories—and this was still done mainly by human hands. Pick and shovel required no diploma; there was work for the unskilled and the illiterate. It was a simple time of no application forms or Social Security cards or suitability tests or pension plans, the lack of which the workingman would feel bitterly one day, but which made the entry to casual work quicker. It was also a time for the small entrepreneur, the pushcart operator, the door-to-door peddler, the sidewalk salesman.

The foreign immigrants, too, were crowded into the worst housing. But cities were still growing in a more or less haphazard way, still mixtures of rich and poor, old and new, all living within sight and sound of each other. In the tightest immigrant slum it was possible to see or hear the ways of older settlements with all the clues these offered to successful living in a metropolis. The foreigner was highly conscious that he was in a new land and needed to learn new ways. He may have come from a city abroad. But his greatest advantage over his native contemporary was the presence of older inhabitants from whom he could learn. The friendly neighbor—or even an unfriendly one —was a powerful figure in the making of new Americans. In the city of fifty years ago, the established Americans could hardly avoid knowing the immigrants were there. People walked. The center of business and industry was down-town. All parts of the city were close at hand and brushing against each other.

The young foreigners went to schools populated by the native-born. From the American children and their teachers the immigrants not only learned the habits and idioms of city living, but they also absorbed the ambitions and standards of normal hope. This was not always a pleas-ant process and integration often came with bitterness and cruelty. But the country recognized that it had masses of newcomers. In the great cities of the East and Midwest no one doubted that the new element in the American population required some reaction from native society. Hundreds of organizations, some from within the immi-grant groups and some from outside, turned to the job of integrating the newcomers with public schools, adult edu-cation, community houses, and systematic visitations by religious groups, private charities, and the local political chieftains.

The modern American immigrant comes to the city at a bad time. The Negro and, to a lesser extent, the white rural migrant encounter discrimination harsher for coming from their own countrymen. From this the white man and

the American Indian can usually retreat. There is a constant shuttling between farm and city, or reservation and
city, in one direction when conditions at home get too
grim, in the other when jobs in the city are too scarce.
But the periodic retreats increase family instability, dis-
rupt education, and prevent serious commitment to making a decent, permanent home. For the Negro there is no
such easy return, since he escapes not only hunger but re-
pression. But other conditions delay his setting down
roots: an even lower level of education than the rural white,
more discrimination against him with jobs and the almost
impermeable barrier that keeps the Negro out of the housing market.

The chief disadvantage for the native migrant is the
erosion of the traditional foothold for the novice in the
metropolis: the unskilled job. The ditchdigger, the factory hand, the street peddler—these were typical roles for
the newcomer starting upward from 1880 to 1920. But
these are the jobs that are now shrinking, to the peculiar
disadvantage of the newcomer to the city who comes
with poor education from an agrarian culture uncon-
cerned with industrial and white collar skills. In factories,
about 1,500,000 jobs a year are abolished by automation.
In construction work between 1956 and 1962 work ac-
complished went up 30 per cent while the number of workers was cut 25 per cent. The open jobs are mostly for skilled
technicians or white collar and managerial positions. The
only place with a consistent increase in available jobs has
been in government and that has been relatively small—
less than 300,000 new positions a year—and most of those
teaching jobs in the public schools. As production-per-man

goes up in industry, the working population continues to go up. In 1965 the number of Americans reaching age eighteen will be 50 per cent higher than in 1960. For the pushcart and door-to-door peddler, the times are bad, too. In 1900 there were 77,000 licensed hucksters and peddlers, but even though licensing and nose-counting are far more complete today, by 1950 there were only 24,000. In a rich economy, success in merchandising comes from volume of sales at low prices. This requires large investment and access to credit. The supermarket and discount house are creatures of this generation and they can undersell the lone proprietor.

The city itself has changed, almost entirely to the disadvantage of the impoverished newcomer. The transition from rural poverty to urban poverty is bewildering under any circumstances. The newcomer probably came from dilapidated farmhouses or shacks in the field without running water or electricity. In 1960 there were still 7,000,000 dwellings, 12 per cent of the total, that lacked running water or a toilet. In the city a gas stove, plaster on the walls, electric wiring, plumbing, rigid rules of trash and garbage disposal may be unfamiliar and seem unimportant. Life in the city is almost always overwhelming. The lifetime face-to-face personal relations of the village are replaced by fast-moving, fast-talking, impatient people in business suits sitting in remote high offices requesting forms in triplicate. Mass transit—subways, multiple bus lines, transfers, endless blocks of huge buildings—can be dizzying. The punctuality and impersonality of city jobs can be depressing. The new legal and social demands for proper clothing and medical care for school children and

the competition on the basis of writing on school applications and job forms and welfare reports, all may seem
mysteries comparable to the language barrier of the earlier
foreigners and, in one way, worse. Most bureaucrats assume that any native-born American can write the mother
tongue, can fill out forms, understand rapidly-uttered
directions in business protocol, and can get around unaided in his own city. It is not a valid assumption. But few
native migrants are willing to admit it. There is a glossary
for the semi-literate—"I don't have my glasses with me,"
or "My hands are dirty, would you please fill it out?" or,
"Oh, was I supposed to bring that paper with me?"
—phrases used not only to avoid admission of difficulty
with writing or reading, but also to avoid the painful moment when a parent has to admit to his own child that he
is illiterate.

The new city deepens all the traditional problems.
Since World War II the experienced city-dwellers have
moved to the suburbs or to new housing developments
away from downtown. With them have gone the big stores,
the supermarkets, many of the factories and office buildings. The private car squeezed mass transit offstage and
prosperous American life accommodated itself to the victor. Homes, stores, working places, even entertainment
(Philadelphia has five downtown theaters but thirty summer suburban ones) all built themselves for the conven-
ience of the automobile rather than for the railroad or bus
or subway or pedestrian. This left the central cores of
cities decayed and abandoned and this is where the newcomers settle. Instead of living interspersed among older

residents, they crowd into whole blocks and entire neighborhoods that have emptied out their original residents en
masse, sometimes in a matter of a few months. This process has broken an important chain of inheritance by which
the accumulated experience of civilized urban living was
normally passed on to the newcomer. Conformity, a curse
to those who have learned the crucial mechanics of living,
serves its purpose in the struggle to master a new environment. A vital part of this learning process is the urge of the
newcomer to adjust to the prevailing standards and to the
expectations of his neighbors. But now there was no prevailing standard, no expectation by anyone, no model to
follow, nothing to adjust to.

Many of the rural migrants had never before lived
under the same roof with another family. Certainly they
had never conducted their total family ritual within chambers that were only a few feet away from a dozen other
chambers where other families were living out their lives,
all without the cleansing action of open land and sun and
wind. The almost automatic conditions of city-life co-
operation—embodied in the commonplace concept of
"the people downstairs" or, also alien to the rural family,
"the people next door"—is slow to come to families who
for generations had space and open fields for neighbors.
The mechanics of tenement living can be awesome, its integration into the unconscious skills of day-to-day living
can take a long time. For many, modern plumbing—the
toilet bowl and water closet, the kitchen sink drain—seems
governed by principles as arcane as those for a nuclear
reactor. Plaster walls seem made for graffiti or for drilling

and exploration, especially by children not yet initiated to winter winds in the North. No hogs or chickens care for the garbage, and it is often unclear who does.

For people raised in a forgiving climate in dwellings that have been immemorially ramshackle, there is little skill in carpentering. It is the old-time urbanite who is the irrepressible handyman. Newcomers to the city will sometimes shiver in cruel cold for lack of a dozen nails and a hammer and an eye for defense against the weather. For those brought up in the ageless shacks of the South, the family shelter is taken for granted as a part of nature, like a tree or a creek, and as unalterable to the unaided hand. The niceties of the city—swept sidewalks and a patch of lawn out front—are alien to those who never had sidewalks and for whom grass was self-tending, like leaves on a tree. In the untypical neighborhoods where old-timers have remained, the newcomers are noticeably quicker to adopt these habits of care for home and neighborhood.

Confusing though his own dwelling may be, the newcomer is even more appalled by the machinery of the city itself. Officialdom, "the law," is a different animal entirely. In the rural preserves there is little recourse to officialdom. "The law" is something to be avoided. But if authority needs to be approached or comes unasked, it is in the form of a flesh-and-blood individual known by name, face, and reputation. In the city, "the law" is far more demanding than in the countryside. It governs the attendance of children at school, their vaccinations, the collection of garbage and trash, condition of the house, operation of electrical wiring and plumbing, behavior of family members, the place and nature of one's work, or more likely, the receipt and expenditure of welfare money. But this more pervasive "law" is not a single authority, nor is it a familiar person, consistent and knowable, but a remote and abstract concoction of formal offices, sheets of paper, and a shifting cast of strangers. It is part of the wave of nervous signals that keep pouring into the newcomer, signals he has never heard before, whose meaning he has trouble comprehending, that he may not even recognize as messages, and that even when recognized as something directed at him he associates with trouble. The older neighbor would have been helpful; but mastery comes only with time and experience. For a surprisingly long time, the unpredictable outside world frightens the rural newcomer. In the disruption of the new life, he clings to the tiny part of this world, his own neighborhood, that he at least knows by sight. This is why there are people more terrified of moving ten blocks than they are of hitchhiking 400 miles. The translation of these weird signals is one service that the experienced neighbor can provide, either by advice or by example. But for vast stretches of today's slums there are no second-generation neighbors, no old hands, friendly or unfriendly. Their absence accelerates the breakdown of order to produce wild and primitive neighborhood conditions, confusion and chaos in the family, wretchedness of lonely individuals. When the latest arrival from the countryside enters the neighborhood, this is all he sees; to the newcomer, as with children, whatever happens is normal. If the novice adjusts to this, he finds himself at war with the outer world. But often he is at war without knowing

it. He finds out only when he is shunned in the fashionable shopping districts or when he goes to school or when
he is arrested.

The schools reflect their neighborhoods. With the
home-owning taxpayers gone, and the articulate city-wise
resident moved away, the district loses its influence in
municipal politics. Street pavements deteriorate, trash col-
lections are missed and rats multiply until they invade the
distant respectable neighborhoods, increasing the dread
of the newcomer. Friendly intercessions with the police by
neighborhood patriarch or priest disappear because the
patriarch has probably moved away and the priest and
minister have followed their parishioners. In the dreary
decline, the most damaging single loss is the neighborhood
school. The building becomes decrepit and the weariest
teachers are assigned to maintain order in them: newcomers have no powerful PTA or organized voting bloc
to threaten aldermen. Primary purpose of the classroom
becomes discipline, which is often genuinely difficult to
impose, partly because the children are untouched by any
spirit of learning, partly because teaching staffs are generally inadequate, and partly because a segment of the
student body already is in fierce revolt. Classroom education is filled with white collar symbols and values and
these usually mean nothing to the slum students, either
in their own experience or in the example of anyone they
know.

The public school has been the social seedbed of
modern American democracy but with a few brilliant ex-
ceptions it is failing in America's central cities. Tradition-
ally the community school has established personal links

among children from different classes and cultures. Even under unsympathetic circumstances, a few irrepressible talents have sprung, obvious and unmistakable, from all cultures represented in a school, a phenomenon that has in its own quiet way contributed to the basic national ethic of respect for the potential of the individual rather than for his class. For the children of the affluent, this has been a deep, if largely unconscious, social lesson. Furthermore, it has forced the middle and upper classes to compete in excellence rather than drift in the complacence of imagined superiority of inherited position. The continuing vigor of American society owes much to this demonstration before the young in their schools. For the children of the poor and deprived, the association in the classroom has meant respect, sometimes grudging, for the possibility of talent and decency among the affluent, and, more important, it has provided the most helpful clues to academic and social achievement. It has been the greatest single bridge for escape from destitution and despair. But the homogeneous school, with all the children from the slums or all from college-degree households, loses that function. The school in the slum has a greater role to play than in any other single kind of neighborhood, for it is the most likely place that the child can find new directions after the culture break with his parents' past, rise above deficiencies at home, and allay the confusion of the unsettled migrant. Yet, these are the most neglected schools in America. James Conant estimates that they spend less than half the money per student and have fewer than half the ratio of teachers to students, compared with schools in affluent districts. The slum school, often the dumping ground for unsatisfactory

teachers, is populated by bewildered, unprepared, and unhappy children who can only re-infect each other with
apathy and confusion.

When the newcomer looks for a job he seldom carries
convincing credentials of experience and training, but
worse, he usually carries the ineffable stigma of his neighborhood. The millions of the poor who are Negroes carry
the extra burden of discrimination against their skin.
This takes from them the technique of quiet success by
which other ethnic groups in the past have overcome prejudice. The Negro has no chance quietly to become a success selling vacuum cleaners door-to-door in the better
neighborhoods, or to fake his way into a white collar job,
or to slip unnoticed into a skilled occupation. The Horatio
Alger tradition applied to the European immigrant called
for the ambitious chap to insinuate himself into a job and
become such a smashing success that he won the admira-
tion of the boss and his fellow-employees before they remembered that all Germans are stupid, all Irish are drunks,
and all Italians are gangsters. For the man with a dark skin
there is no such bypass of the stereotype.

It has been a long time, in the memory of contempo-
raries, since the mass migrations from Europe. In the
1920's the immigration gates were closed except for the
precisely selected people whose education and skills were
pre-scheduled. In the meantime, the country convinced
itself that poverty has disappeared. Societies to help newcomers are long gone or evolved into something else. The
settlement houses are either torn down or are splendid
edifices in established neighborhoods, though some have
lately been responding to the old sounds of need. In the

place of the immigrant societies and the patronizing politi-
cians have come the welfare agencies, which in terms of
cash do more than any settlement house or ward heeler
ever did and have prevented mass starvation and political
chaos. But they are not humanity expressed so much as
humanity administered. They are indispensable but they
are not enough. Fewer children in the slums starve or freeze
than in the 1890's, but fewer are recognized by name and
face by someone from the outside world.

There is a final irony for the newly arrived poor in the
cities. It costs them more to be poor than it used to. Living
standards are higher, not only in the expectation of the
community, but of the law. The number of persons per
room, the temperature of the house in winter, the stability
of stairways, the dental and medical condition of school
children—often honored in the breach—are nevertheless
regulated by law and one way or another the poor pay for
it. These are good things for the law to demand, but for the
benefits provided they complicate the economy of poverty in the city (rural areas are usually devoid of such law
and of welfare). The greatest complication of all is the
domination of the American economy by the automobile.
Public transportation between the centers of human ac-
tivity has shrivelled. The poor no longer live in the shadow
of the majority of jobs. There are fewer garment shops
whose owners can be charmed, or foundry foremen to nag,
or shoe factories to hang around. These are dispersed over
the landscape where there is free parking, along with the
supermarkets with the cheapest prices. But few of the
poor can get to them. The poor today are stranded in an
island of slums surrounded by indifference.

The indifference is no unique callousness among Americans. Americans, in fact, are less inured to the suffering of others than most established peoples. They still long, happily, to do something about tragedy. But poverty has never been pleasant to look at and the average citizen, even of a humane society, does not actively seek it out. When cities were mixtures of differing economic groups, living cheek by jowl, and a man going to work walked by the poor, or perhaps saw them at the downtown employment office, or had his children sit next to their children in school, there was no choice. The middle-class citizen knew there was poverty because it was in the next block, or he saw it from the trolley, or he saw men selling buttons or repairing umbrellas in the street. The middle-class man may have protected himself with a smug explanation of why this happened, but he knew it existed. Today the middle-class American lives in the suburbs or in an entirely different part of the city. He does not usually have to go daily through the central city, or at least not through the littered streets behind the big hotels. He is much more apt to move outward to the fringes for working and shopping. He and his children may go for years without ever seeing a slum. (Indeed, the socially conscious parent in the city has been known to take his children on a deliberate tour of the slums to open young eyes to what exists in his own community.) His highways loop around or leap over these distant anonymous blocks at sixty miles an hour.

Thirty years ago two-thirds of the population of the United States was in serious economic trouble. Today a smaller proportion of Americans is poor, not so small as the affluent seem to think, but small enough to drop below the threshold of national consciousness. Because they are miserable out in the distant farmlands and mountains or in their cramped slums in the abandoned cores of cities, the poor are poor all by themselves.

Besides, the poor used to look poor and very often they don't any more. For centuries the literature of poverty was filled with words like "rags" and "faded" and "torn." This was the state of clothing among the poor until American poverty became the best-dressed in the world. In recent years clothes have become casual and dyes have become perfect.

It was possible recently to watch a girl at a dance in a Chicago community house, in a pink cotton dress with a bright blue bow at the collar; she could have been picked up by a parent in a big car and gone home to an apartment with a doorman. A boy in chinos and sports shirt walked down a San Francisco street with books under his arm; he might have entered a hillside villa without raising eyebrows. It would be an imprudent man who bet on the income level of the children's families. The Chicago girl went to a dark and uriniferous stairway beside a gin mill and walked into her tenement where drunken adults yelled at her and babies in cribs cried to be changed. The boy in San Francisco went up a back fire escape to a dingy pair of rooms where his husbandless mother fed her children from cold cans. The dyes in American clothing do not fade and in their fidelity they have removed from the streets one of the historic clues to poverty.

Paradoxically, the poor in America of the 1960's are materially better off than the impoverished of the past, but they are poor nonetheless and they may be poorer in spirit. As we shall see, they are unnourished by their native countryside, so they have become refugees in the cities where they are hidden from their own countrymen, sustained by welfare payments that keep them fed and clothed, but for the most part without hope of deliverance. The American city which once demonstrated for the world how to receive masses of penniless newcomers and from them produce a generation of productive citizens seems to have forgotten how it did it.

CHAPTER THREE

"But $40 don't pay for a house, a kid, and a car."

"You mean you want to take a look at a hillbilly!"

Homer Burleigh, thirty-three, from Anniston, Alabama, hefty, freckle-faced and sandy-haired, dressed in T-shirt, dark slacks, loafers, and for the moment immobile with resentment, blocked the doorway to his flat. Like 20,000 other Southern whites living in the two and one-half square miles of Chicago's Uptown, he had his pride, his problems, and an innate suspicion of the Eastern city slicker.

Homer Burleigh finds it hard to stay angry for long and he led the way inside. Four of his five children, ages two, three, five, and seven (a ten-year-old boy was still in school), ran about in bare feet, dressed only in underpants. Mrs. Burleigh, a wan, hard, very pregnant woman, also was barefooted. The five-year-old boy chanted to the visitor, *"You got on a necktie. You got on a necktie."*

He walked into a small kitchen, sat down, rubbed a large hand over his face and sighed. He was in trouble and he knew it and he was, after the first resentment, anxious to talk about it. His trouble was not just the meagreness whose clues lay about: the drab four rooms, a living room with two pieces of furniture—television set and, opposite,

29

old sofa; two bedrooms with four beds for seven people; the "extra room," a horrid chamber painted throughout—ceiling, walls, closet, doors—in a mottled grey and black; and a back room with a good kitchen table and four chairs, refrigerator, and kitchenette. Homer Burleigh was penniless, about to be evicted, maybe even jailed. Much of this was his own fault, the panicked response to crises. But basically he was living through the recurring ritual of the poor in which they are reminded that theirs are fragile, leaky vessels in the sea of life, barely able to keep afloat with the best of luck and in danger of sinking with the slightest storm. Homer Burleigh made mistakes when the margin of safety with which he had to live permitted no mistakes whatever.

On one side there was the Burleigh family, which had not done so badly. A complete country boy who hadn't finished the fourth grade had gone to the city and from nothing made himself a skilled industrial worker with respectable wages. On the other side was the turbulent social sea from which they tried constantly to escape—the Uptown world of Chicago, reminder of the probability of poverty. This was the urban world of the Southern white and the refugee from Appalachia.

A walk through it shows the transient desperation. Families of four live in one room at $25 a week. A single man can rent a room for $1 a night if he wears plain slacks and sport shirt or $1.75 if he has on a suit, $7 if he has a girl. A broken down building bears a sign, OLD AGE WELFARE PENSIONERS WELCOME—WILL MOVE YOU IN FREE. Some of the buildings are locally famous. One had a fire that killed five people, including three children. Another on Winthrop Avenue for a time had a tenant who was a Hatfield of the Hatfields-and-McCoys and when he was visited by a local city worker Mr. Hatfield said coldly, *"I don't want nothing to do with no smooth-shaven Northerner."* One three-story tenement had a fire in which nobody was killed, somehow, but which resulted in the discovery that eighty-two children lived there. A city youth worker checked on a boy in a playground team and found him a member of a family of thirteen living in a basement apartment with a constantly flooded floor, feces and garbage, the smell of sewer gases, charred walls from a number of aborted fires from bad electrical wiring—$130 a month.

Sixty per cent of the people in the rooming houses have been at their address for less than a year. One landlord complained that he was losing money on the building he had owned and tended all his life; a curious outsider checked the real estate records and found the building had been constructed in 1925 with apartments for six families, that it was long since paid for, and he found that there were now twenty-eight mailboxes in the hallway. Children don't go out much because they are relatively new to the neighborhood and to the city or their parents are fearful. Underneath the nearby elevated train platform are strings of abandoned automobiles where police are supposed to keep out street walkers and amateur sex parties. The kids in the neighborhood are no better or worse to begin with but the odds are against them, as they are against their parents. A city youth worker thinks he has known about five hundred families in Uptown during the three years he has worked there but he has never known a child to go on to college. From this fearsome sea Homer Burleigh shrank, but it seemed ready to draw him and his family into the depths.

Homer Burleigh has an engaging charm and it is easy to see him shrugging off life's blows. They began early.

To begin with, he was born in a poor region into a poor family in a dying occupation. His father was a share-cropper in Alabama. His mother died when he was three. He did not get along with his stepmother; he quit school before he finished the fourth grade. When he was seventeen he left his father's house, which was dominated by his stepmother and her three daughters, and went to live with an uncle in town who worked in a small industrial plant. Then his uncle lost his job and went looking for work in Detroit, so young Homer went with him.

In Detroit, Homer stood in line for work at the Budd plant and when finally the man barked, "*What kind of work?*" Homer remembered a sign that had said, "Punch press operators needed," so he said,

"*Punch press.*"

The man looked up, perhaps because of the Alabama drawl. "*You ever work a punch press before?*"

Homer said, "*No, Sir, I never did.*"

"*Then how come you're asking for a job doing it?*"

"*Well, I want a job.*" Homer is a man easy to like. He got the job.

For a year he took to his boarding house room between $80 and $120 a week, fabulous pay for a country boy. At least half of it went every week on gay parties with girl friends and weekend gambling. When the work week was cut down and take-home pay was only $70 he went looking for a new job. Homer was never the type to wither on the vine. He was a go-getter, the way a man is supposed to be when he is climbing upward. Having faked his way into a punch press job, he now pretended to be an experienced cook and took over a boarding house at $300 pay a month plus free room and meals. Homer thinks his meals were quite good; it is not possible to obtain a more objective judgment. This time he cut down on the fun and games until he had $3000 saved in a sock in his dresser drawer. When he had an even $3000, about a year later, he bought a 1940 Chevrolet and headed back for Anniston where he cut a mighty swath. *"Between me and the car and a few good-looking women, the $3000 didn't last ten months."*

He was back living with his father again, doing odd jobs around town. But there were too many fights. One morning he washed his best chinos in well water, laid them in the sun, and when they were dry put them on, got out a clean sports shirt and told his stepmother, *"Tell Dad it might be a year or two before I come back."*

In Pontiac, Michigan he stood in line for five hours and at closing time still hadn't reached the hiring window. The next day he appeared at 3 a.m. *"There were already six men ahead of me."* He got a punch press job where he made $1.80 an hour with about $85 a week take-home pay.

The Horatio Alger instinct was irrepressible. One day he saw a notice on the bulletin board that they were hiring buffers at $2.21. He told his foreman he was going to apply. *"What makes you think you're a buffer?"* the foreman asked.

"Two dollars and twenty-one cents," said Homer in his slow, nasal drawl.

The plant was producing the 1955 Pontiac and Homer was given the job of smoothing the raw front fender on a buffing wheel, requiring careful abrasion of the curved surface but not too long in one place because the heat would make the metal buckle. The foreman dubiously turned Homer over to an experienced buffer, a Negro from Meridian, Mississippi. Homer jauntily took up his first fender and burned a hole right through the metal. He looked curtly at the hole in the metal, chucked the fender back in a box, and started walking away. *"Where you going?"* the Negro asked.

"I'm quitting before they fire me," Homer said. Homer put his arms up on his kitchen table as he recalled the day in the Pontiac plant.

"That colored boy he said to me, 'You come on back here and do what I say. Now pick up another fender and hold it just like this'—he took one and made me take one and grab it the way he did—'and you hold it just like a baby, and rock it back and forth, back and forth, gentle but fast, just like a baby.' Well, I began doing all right. I spoiled a couple after that but the colored guy fixed them up for me."

So the white man from Anniston, Alabama, with the help of a fellow immigrant from Meridian, Mississippi, learned to be a buffer and took home well over $100 a week. When the Pontiac plant shut down for change of models, the Negro, typically, waited workless in Michigan; he felt he had no place to go back to. But Homer, typically for the Southern white man, headed back to Anniston.

Back in Alabama Homer was driving a dump truck for $40 a week when he met Millicent, a waitress with a two-year-old son from a previous marriage. *"I decided I wanted her and the kid. But $40 don't pay for a house, a kid, and a car."*

It is significant that everywhere in Homer's plan there was a car. This is normal for almost any American male. It was more intense for the wandering man on the way up, for a car represents not only social status, but in a mobile society it means freedom, privacy, pursuit of work, and the ability to go home if there is no work. There has quietly evolved a generation of Americans who feel self-consciously exposed in a railroad coach or a bus and for whom the only self-respecting transportation is in one's own private vehicle. And, indeed, so much of the country has adapted itself to this—factories as well as stores and apartments—that by now the car represents the only practical way to get to many jobs and homes.

The trip North with Millicent—her mother would care for her son for a short time—was in a 1951 sky-blue Studebaker with a new black top, financed with the help of $100 borrowed from Homer's uncle. They were headed for Detroit but in a Nashville gasoline station Homer noticed a car at a neighboring pump. It was an impressive Oldsmobile with Illinois plates. *"How things in Illinois?"* he asked the man.

"Oh, pretty good," the Oldsmobile owner said. *"What you looking for?"*

"*My wife and me are going up looking for work,*" Homer told him.

The man had a Chicago *Tribune* on the front seat and offered it to him. "*Look at the want ads if you want to.*" And that's how the Burleighs happened to become Chicagoans. Four days after they arrived in Chicago Homer was making $110 a week doing piecework on a punch press.

Life was good in Chicago, or as good as he expected it to be. Millicent was confused by much of the city, but she was resourceful in getting meals and making do in furnished flats. Homer was a good worker and on piecework he turned out profitable quantities.

Neither one of them can remember just when or how the change occurred but sometime between that first week seven years before and the day Homer sat at the kitchen table and told about it, their lives took a downturn. For one thing, they had four children, which with Millicent's son, made a household of seven. Expenses began to climb, in lurches with each child. They needed a bigger apartment than the neat three-room flat they had the first year and this meant more furniture. As their needs went up for more bedrooms, they were pushed into a category of apartment that is in short supply, which meant that they began drifting downward in quality of neighborhood and of building. Medical bills, which they never had considered a normal running expense, somehow became a constant drain, at first just for the deliveries and then for baby illnesses.

There was no single period when these problems emerged into their consciousness. But it bore down on them in the late 1950's when business took a turn for the worse. Homer felt it in the machine shop where he worked.

The men were cut back on hours a week, Homer being among the first to suffer because it was a relatively small shop with men of more seniority in it. When he was cut back to three days a week he couldn't pay for his rent and food and everlasting car payments.

So despite the urging of his boss to stay on a little longer until business improved, Homer struck out for another job that would pay a full week's work. He found one at once. Again he did well because he is a hard worker and an engaging fellow with initiative and a certain brassy friendliness. But when the new shop cut down on the workweek, Homer was among the first to feel the reduction because he was the most recently hired. He left for another shop to get a full week's work. In each place his lack of seniority made him the first hit by reduced time. A home economist could have told Homer that he simply didn't earn enough money to support a family of seven properly and an ingenious one might even have drawn a curve to show precisely when the Burleigh fertility outran the Burleigh income. All Homer knew was that no matter what he did, he didn't have enough money. Yet he was trying as hard as ever.

He was working in a machine shop making $85 a week, when the sores began. These were strange running sores, first under his arm and then in his groin. Even before this he knew he was facing a financial crisis of some sort. His take-home pay was about $300 a month. Rent took $110 of this. The car, by now a 1954 Pontiac, took $60 a month. This left $130 for everything else, which for a family of seven is not enough for the most economical complete diet.

Yet he also had to extract from this amount clothes, gasoline and oil, medical care.

He shifted to a plastic molding plant where, for a time, the take-home pay was higher, but it, too, sagged down to about $300 a month. He began falling behind on his car payments. Then he claims he lost his car-payment booklet with his receipts, showing he had paid $400 of the total of $1200, and when the finance company reissued a new book it showed him owing the full $1200. The finance company threatened to attach his pay. His sores gave him more and more trouble and got infected from the dust in the plastic factory. A doctor told him he'd have to stop that kind of work. At this point he committed folly. He applied for a new Social Security number under which to get his pay, thus, he thought, escaping the clutches of the finance company. He says the finance company then seized the car on the street but told Homer he still owed them $1200.

It is difficult to be sure what did happen. Homer is a hard worker but he is not a creature of cold rationality. He is not too hard on himself in the car episode and he may have been all wrong. But car dealers and finance companies have perpetrated documented frauds on the innocent immigrants and on some not so innocent. Welfare workers, for example, confirmed the case of a Mexican-American from Texas who bought a six-year-old car that had a true value of about $400. The dealer charged him $800 for it, plus a flat $240 carrying charge, plus ordinary finance company interest on the whole amount, including the carrying charge and $120 insurance that they took out for him. He had made four monthly payments of $75 each and had paid $200 for a set of four new tires when he had an accident, rolled over, and ruined another car. He was in the hospital when he learned that the finance company had claimed the wreck, declared it a total loss (although the new tires presumably were usable), and threatened court action to recover all the money the man allegedly owed. At the same time lawyers for the man whose car the Mexican-American had ruined, brought suit because the $120 for insurance was for collision only, not for liability. The finance company protected their interest in the car but not the owner's.

Homer Burleigh, car gone, job almost gone, finally turned to welfare, for the first time after seven years in the city. The welfare worker told him it would be two weeks before the payments would start, so Homer worked out the two weeks. His welfare came to $261 a month and this would not pay the rent and food for them all, so from time to time toward the end of the month, Millicent would go to a nearby Presbyterian Church for free food.

The wheels of bureaucracy turned. Six months after the welfare payments started Homer was notified that he would lose his payments and would be charged with fraud. He thought they had caught up with his new Social Security number. But they had not. He was charged with having received unreported pay while getting welfare. He had. It was the pay for the last two weeks of work, after he had applied for aid to dependent children but before the payments began. The day he talked at the kitchen table, the last of the final welfare payment had been spent and in four days he was to be evicted from his flat for non-payment of rent.

"If the arm continues this way, and if they don't give me assistance, I'm going to have to put the kids in a home." His eyes filled. *"These kids are young. They don't know all these problems. But that older boy, he's pretty bright. You can't keep things from him forever. Anyway, we haven't been able to pay the rent and Monday is the end. When they move us onto the sidewalk, the kids will know, all right."*

And so the lines of failure seemed to converge for Homer Burleigh: a motherless home full of contention, almost no formal education, an impoverished landscape to grow in with no hope for a young man, a pattern of wandering to where there was money without making a permanent commitment, a drifting of life without heed for the consequences of more children. But he was not an evil man, nor a lazy one. His was simply the fragile vessel of endemic poverty, never strong enough to withstand a prolonged storm. And his children seemed doomed to go forth in a similarly brittle craft.

The plight of the Burleighs seemed ultimate, an emergency that needed immediate attention. A few blocks away, in a city office of the Youth Commission, a cigar-smoking worker who had seen several hundred emergencies agreed. But time had taught him that as one got increasingly desperate, one tolerated a smaller margin of safety.

"Middle class people think they've got an emergency if they can't pay the grocer," he said. *"Poor people don't think they've got an emergency until they've got no groceries."*

By chance a confirming telephone call came in. He leaned back in his chair, listening, his cigar still. He covered the mouthpiece of the phone with his palm and told his partner in the office, "*It's the Mayfields. They don't have any food for the weekend. Not a thing, they say.*" He turned back to the telephone and said to the Mayfields:

"*Try Goudy School. They had some food for distribution earlier this week.*"

His partner waved his hand violently and said, "*Goudy's all out.*"

The cigar smoker said to the telephone, "*No. No. I'm told Goudy's all out of food. How about the church down on the avenue, the Protestant church? They don't have any, either? Well, I'll tell you what to do. You try Father Maguire at the big Catholic Church on the other side of your block. Remember now, Father Maguire, not Father Landers. Father Maguire may have some. If he hasn't call me back. Yeh, okay. Good luck.*"

He put the phone down, and lit his cigar.

"*I'm not too worried about them. His mother's on welfare so I know she's got some dough and he's got a married sister on ADC so they'll have some food. It isn't as though they had no place to go.*"

CHAPTER FOUR

"Daddy, I'll step out
and maybe something will happen..."

Willie Johnson is a short, stocky West Virginian with powerful shoulders and a large head, laconic manner, and a peculiar memory for dates. He is fifty-five years old, which means that in the eyes of society he has at least seven more years of active wage earning before he qualifies for a Social Security pension. In his own mind, too, he is ready for more work. He went into the coal mines when he was thirteen years old and he kept at it steadily in the manner of the region where hard daily labor is considered the only honorable state of man. Willie Johnson, in the past, permitted few things to interfere with the profound rhythm of work. A runaway mine locomotive "on September 11, 19-and-25" crushed him against a pit wall but twenty days later he walked out of the hospital and back into the mine.

Twelve years ago he was earning more than $100 every week. Today he earns zero. He will probably never work again. He won't work again because in all of his county there is no work for him to do.

The go-getting response is: "If a man looks hard enough, he will find *some* work."

This may be true, but it is hard to believe in Logan

County. If it is true, it applies to a tiny fragment of any human group, to the indomitably ambitious, the unusually resilient, the extraordinary men who can have an entire career collapse and at precisely that moment take the initiative to abandon the other supports of social man— friends, family, institutions, the land of their birth. And if such men do seek out jobs in new places, they either have money to move their families for the search or they can bring themselves to leave wife and children behind to face the unknown at home while they disappear to face the unknown afar. But what of the men who are merely average?

God help the man who is only an average human being in Logan County, West Virginia. This is one of the 230 counties of southern Appalachia, the beautiful mountain region from West Virginia to northern Alabama, where 7,000,000 Americans are gasping from economic suffocation. Today they live in crumbling shacks, sitting idle all day, eating inadequate food. Are they all deficient human beings? Are they poor because they are lacking ordinary qualities, or has something happened beyond their control?

They live in a land of melancholy beauty, with steep hills and wooded valleys scarred by the spill of old mines. The roads run by sagging shacks hung with galvanized wash basins. Near Charleston's urban radiations there are the common paradoxes: the heavy television antenna mounted on a pole in the ground because the family shack is not strong enough to support it. But as the city recedes so do its reflections of television and of money. The shacks become shabbier, the electric refrigerators disappear from the front porches, and then the electric wires themselves. Pumps and privies show up in the back yards. The roads bear a rash of potholes, the poverty pox of poor counties. The neatest manmade structure for miles is a large sign freshly painted in tasteful green and white: THE NEXT NINE MILES IS THE PROPERTY OF THE DUNGESS RUM COAL COMPANY.

The human figures in the landscape have a stubborn pride. Like the unemployed miner who got a lucky day's work and took his old black lunch pail, symbol of masculinity and usefulness, and at lunchtime retired to a corner where some of the men saw that all it contained were potato peelings. The potatoes remained at home for the family.

They are inheritors of a long history of self-reliance. Eighty years ago a father among these mountain people still made all the shoes for his children. The family food was grown around the house. But life has become more complicated. Families can live not by their own sweat alone, but need cash money also. And in all of Appalachia the three main ways of making money—farming, lumbering, mining—need fewer and fewer men with each passing year. In 1948 one American miner produced six tons of bituminous coal a day. Today he produces fourteen tons. Both the companies and the unions strive for machines that will produce still more coal with still fewer men, in a desperate dilemma. It is Logan County coal that heats the members of Congress in their work, part of their work being to struggle with the problems of unemployment and automation. If Logan County coal becomes less automated and cheap than coal from other counties, the Capitol, in conventional fiscal prudence, will take its business elsewhere, thus deepening the problem of unemployment and automation in Logan County.

Coal, for all practical purposes, is the only source of money in Logan County and when Willie Johnson last worked in 1954 there were 14,000 men in the mines. Now there are 3500 men and nothing has come to take the place of the mines. What do you do if suddenly your life work is not needed? Or worse, not suddenly, but bit by bit, always with hope, a hint, an insistence that you will go back again?

A professional man in Logan County who earns $7500 a year described what happened to one coal miner who ten years ago was earning $5700 a year (which in current dollars would be in the general salary range of the professional man):

"This bachelor used to make good money in the mines until he got laid off. He's got no family so he gets no welfare aid for dependent children. He's not crippled or chronically ill so he gets no other kind of welfare. He's not sixty so he gets no Mine Workers pension and of course he's not sixty-two so he gets no Social Security. He's one of those unlucky ones who's healthy and has no dependent children: ineligible for any aid at all. I let him sleep in my woodshed and he does odd jobs around the house. Some old friends of his who are still in the mines let him do odd jobs when they can. My wife and I give him some food when we know he's had no odd jobs for a long time. Things get pretty grim for him. But he's a lot better off than some men who live in abandoned shacks out in the woods."

Willie Johnson has a seventeen-year-old son, Willie Jr., a handsome, unhappy youth who has combed the county for jobs, any job at any price. He is competing with hungry family men and roving hermits, all of them scouring the citizenry for temporary crumbs from other people's incomes.

When he was in the ninth grade, young Willie was called aside by his father one August evening.

"Willie, I don't believe I can send you to school this year. I can't send you and the little ones, too, and they just have to go."

The son replied, *"Daddy, I'll step out and maybe something will happen and I can go back later on."*

Nothing happened.

"In school the kids have to buy books, they got to buy lunches or take them and they got to have clothes," the father said.

It costs about $28 a year for books in the secondary grades in the irony of many public schools: the rich districts provide texts and other services free to students already skilled in academic and social techniques from their family life; the poor districts charge their students for books, students for whom the school is the only place they will ever learn to survive in a white collar world.

The federally-supported hot lunch, the only balanced meal most children in Logan County get, costs 50 cents a day in the upper grades. These are precisely the children who need a hot lunch and precisely the ones for whose parents 50 cents a day is a grave expense. Nevertheless, the children could take a lunch from home. Sandwiches for five children, one is told, take a lot of bread and filling, more than the budget can stand. Then why don't the children eat at school what they would eat at home? *"How*

*you going to ask a kid to take beans and potatoes for lunch?
If they's going to have beans or anything else for lunch."*

School also means clothes. Luckily clothes are casual in the United States but even the usual school clothes—untorn shoes, slacks and sport shirt for boys; sneakers, socks, blouse and skirt for girls—cost "extra" money.

Perhaps $28 a year would not stop a fiercely devoted scholar, nor lack of lunch, nor even ragged clothes in class. But the fiercely devoted scholar is not usual. And consider what it means to the Johnson family, with five children in school, to pay $28 a year for books, $2.50 a week per student for lunch, and a set of clothes.

The total family budget for Mr. and Mrs. Johnson and their eight children is $165 a month. It is the Federal aid-to-dependent children, administered by the local county and under its rules the highest family payment possible. From this the Johnsons pay $27 a month rent, for which they get a former company cottage of four rooms with no running water except for the copious amounts that come through the roof when it rains. They pay $7.50 a month for electricity which goes mostly for their stove and refrigerator, appliances from their affluent past. To keep the electricity bill low they cook over an open fire in the back yard whenever possible. This leaves $130.50 for everything else. For a family of ten, $130 a month means food.

Shopping is in a nearby small store. To be without an automobile costs the American family a certain amount of social status, which the analyzers of the middle class like to dwell on. But for the poor, in addition to the symbolic loss, there is the very real disadvantage that they cannot often get to supermarkets where prices are lower, the choice of goods wider, the packages larger, and where there are weekly bargains. Most low-cost family budgets are based on careful buying at the cheapest prices, but for the poor this may be impossible.

"First two weeks we have it right smart," Willie Johnson says of the family diet.

When the welfare check comes in they walk down to the store and load up—sacks of flour, corn meal, condensed milk, bags of pinto beans, pecks of potatoes, fryers. For breakfast those first two weeks they have eggs and "soft" bacon with brown gravy. For lunch, a bowl of beans. For supper *"sometimes she'll fry up two chickens for us,"* and they have some potatoes. For those first two weeks there is a glass of milk each day for the younger children.

Then in the last half of the month, in an ebbing tide known to millions of American poor, the food begins to peter out. In the third week the Johnsons may have breakfasts of eggs with brown gravy and a bowl of beans for lunch. *"For supper one day we'll have beans and fried potatoes and next night beans and boiled potatoes. Next night she may make bean cakes. She's pretty good at all the ways she can cook beans."*

The last week? It all depends. The $130 left each month after rent and electricity represents 43 cents a day per person for food. The Department of Agriculture estimates that the lowest-cost adequate diet for a family of ten, based on sophisticated shopping with nutrients in mind, will cost $224 a month. An "emergency" diet will cost $185 a month. This assumes that 100 per cent of the food purchased is eaten, but some surveys show that there is a 20 per cent loss in cooking wastage. So if all the $130 goes for food, the Johnsons still get far from an adequate intake of food. But something almost always happens. Because they live at the edge of adequate nutrition, a pair of new shoes is, for the poor, an economic catastrophe.

"Sometimes we can manage $10, $15 every two or three months on clothes for the kids," Willie Johnson says. *"You know kids' shoes. You can get them for $4 a pair made out of stuff like cardboard and the first rainstorm they're gone. You got to pay $8 for a kid's pair of shoes if they's going to last. Right now four of my kids in school need shoes so bad if they don't get them they can't go to school no more."*

This was obvious before he mentioned it. One boy had leather shoes with uppers opened like a tulip, held onto his feet with string. Another had red plastic overshoes serving as regular footwear, but one of these was ripped from top to sole. The pretty thirteen-year-old daughter returned from school, walking along the roadside looking like a calendar illustration of the typical teen-age girl, dressed in low sneakers, clean white socks, bright blue cotton skirt, and red blouse. It was not until she stepped onto the porch that one could see the ragged holes in her sneakers, only a few threads holding them together.

Consider, therefore, the economics of shoes for the poor. After rent and electricity, the entire Johnson budget will not buy an adequate diet. Any non-food emergency, like shoes, can come only out of the already-deficient meals. At maximum, if the Johnsons each have three meals a day for the whole month, they will have an average of only 14½ cents to spend per person per meal. One pair of the cheapest shoes represents the loss of twenty-eight meals a month. The $8 shoes would last far longer than two pairs of the flimsy $4 ones. But a pair of $8 shoes represent the loss of fifty-six meals. The actual need at the moment, to keep the Johnson children in school and their parents clear of the truancy law, is four pairs of shoes. If the flimsy shoes are bought the food loss is 110 meals that month; if the "sensible" $8 shoes the loss is 220 meals, or 25 per cent of the family's monthly food intake. These are not just theoretical equivalents. They are simple, inescapable substitutions, shoes for food.

This equation demonstrates two rules in the bitter arithmetic of the poor.

One, the poor cannot afford to spend money wisely. The long-lasting $8 shoes make obvious sense in terms of economical footwear, but to exercise such "sense" involves the excruciating decision to sacrifice one quarter of everyone's meals. The same rule applies to everything the poor buy. They seldom see daily newspapers (the cost is ten to fifteen meals a month) and this is one of the many ways the poor lose contact with the larger community. As a practical matter, it means the housewife is out of touch with grocery sales, the supermarket bargains when chicken or pork or beef hit the low points in their price cycles. They are probably out of range of a supermarket, anyway, being without a car, and thus they fall back on the small variety stores. The "giant economy" packages, when they are genuinely economical, are the privilege of families with surplus income to buy in quantity and store for the future. The Johnsons have no surplus.

Two, expenses that are incidental or annoying to

ordinary families are the harshest possible sacrifices for the poor.

When the poor spend money on clothing, doctors, school books, house repairs, or "recreation," there is, usually, only one place it can come from—the withholding of food from already malnourished bodies. Such an expense is that cruel and unnoticed burden on the poor, the sales tax. This is a "painless" tax paid out in pennies with each retail purchase in thirty-six states and the District of Columbia, often promoted as "democratic" because everyone pays the same. It is a nuisance for the average family. It is a device that concentrates sacrifice with merciless accuracy on low income families.

For average-and-above families, the majority of income is spent for things like medical care, insurance, rent, plumbing, gasoline, vacations, and other expenditures not subject to retail sales taxes. For the poor, almost all their income is spent for food and clothing, the focus of most sales taxes.

West Virginia, in the multiple irony of the sales tax, has a high sales tax, a flat 3 per cent on all retail sales and utility bills, and is among the highest states in proportion of family income subject to the tax. This high tax rate on low-income expenditures is to help support its heavy welfare load for low-income families.

Yet, especially in West Virginia, the degree of sacrifice is dramatically different for the poor. By Internal Revenue Service calculations, the average West Virginia family pays about $67.50 a year in sales taxes, a rate of 1.4%. The Johnsons pay $49.80 a year, or 2.5%, almost double. For the average family, the $5.63 in sales taxes a month represents the cost of gasoline for a long Sunday drive. For the Johnsons, $4.15 a month represents a cheap pair of shoes or twenty-nine meals. In West Virginia, one-fifth of all families have a lower income than the Johnsons and for them the sales tax represents glasses of milk from their children; for the average family it means gasoline from their car.

The economics of incidental costs like textbooks also can be calculated directly in meals. The $28 a year for textbooks for each child represents 193 meals a year, but it must come at one time, at the start of the school year, at a time when meals are disappearing for clothes.

The hot lunch program at school is one of those nutritional bargains the poor often cannot afford. Each child who takes advantage of it takes from the rest of the family twenty-five meals a month. Not many families analyze their budgets in these terms. There is a simple method that does it for them. If they buy all the food they can to approach an adequate diet, there is nothing left.

So when "something happens"—new shoes, trousers, a doctor in the house—the menu for the last week of the month is beans and gravy for breakfast, no lunch, and beans and gravy for supper. The night I was with the Johnsons, supper was a purple bubbling mass in a saucepan: canned blackberries picked in the hills the summer before, mixed with flour. It was supper for ten. The date was March 25 and there were still six days to go before the next welfare check. And the problem of the four pairs of shoes had not yet been solved.

Both Mr. and Mrs. Johnson show the shape of most American poverty. They are overweight. They eat cheap carbohydrates—flour, rice, hominy, macaroni, corn meal—

whose bulk for filling the stomach and preventing hunger pangs is the cheapest available. It, with dried beans, is the only major category of food whose consumption per household goes up dramatically in American households as family income goes down. A 1955 Department of Agriculture study shows that households with over $10,000 income used less than four pounds of flour and cereal grain products a week; those with $2000 income used almost 8 pounds a week; and those with less than $1000 income used more than 12 pounds a week. These are good providers of protein, calories, iron, and thiamine, but they are bought instinctively to fill the stomach at lowest cost. And because they constitute such a large part of the total diet of the Johnsons they leave deficiencies in the more expensive nutrients like Vitamin A, calcium, and ascorbic acid. This is one important reason that two-thirds of all urban families with less than $2000 income fail to meet adequate nutritional standards.

As with so much in poverty, one inadequacy—food— leads to another—poor performance in school and work. The missing nutrients weaken the physical and nervous ability of the poor to overcome their problems. The unemployed adult, unnaturally idle, is not sufficiently active to work off such a burden of carbohydrates and he begins to get fat. The excess weight is wearying, compounding the deterioration of unused muscle. Being fat becomes a social burden as well, further robbing him of self-esteem and fixing his image as a less attractive worker. The lack of important nutrients affects body chemistry, reducing resistance to infection, especially in skin and the mucous membranes. The poor are noticeably more prone to colds, pneu-

monia, tuberculosis, and skin diseases. The runny nose is
the poor child's specialty. The nervous system and muscu-
lar reactions lose precision in response. The excess weight
and inefficient body chemistry produce irritability, lack of
energy, and progressive diseases. Insurance companies,
which the poor can seldom patronize, say that overweight
adults are heavy sufferers from diabetes, cirrhosis of the
liver, appendicitis, chronic nephritis, cerebral hemorrhage,
gallbladder disease, and heart ailments.

Poverty at the doorstep of starvation and death takes
the shape of the shrunken body with protruding ribs. But
the next higher step in poverty, typical of the American
phenomenon, is the product of cheap fillers of the stomach
and this shape is fat or obese.

For the children, their bodies still active and burning
up carbohydrates in the urge to grow, there is not usually
obesity. But they are undernourished by American standards, and undernourished for the efficiency and attentiveness required by modern pressures in education. They are
not yet socially affected by obesity, as their parents may be,
nor generally exhibiting the medical symptoms, but in a
sense their dietary weakness is worse for being nascent and
subtle. If they were visibly and dramatically diseased, they
would be treated and accommodated, in most cities. But
instead they are caught in the vague and intricate combination of faulty body chemistry and poor psychological mo-
tivation and this appears as apathy, laziness, inability to
concentrate, and impatience.

W. P. Phipps is principal of the Davy Junior High
School in Davy, West Virginia, and when a Federal program increased the food allocation of welfare families by

about one-third he said the effects in school were dramatic. *"I have seen boys and girls come to school hundreds of times without food and some ashamed to eat the lunches that were prepared from the food that was furnished. These pupils were undernourished and as a result they were listless and dull in school. Those in school whose parents were not on relief vastly outshone the others in school work and other activities. Since the Food Stamp Program has come to our county, I have found this to have changed immensely. Under this program, the people who receive the food stamps have been able to have such a variety in their diets that the children have become more alert in school and can hold their own with the rest in their academic work. They are no longer listless and without hope."*

The Johnsons, already getting the maximum family welfare, still run out of food at the end of most months. Why don't they plan ahead? Why don't they stretch what food there is evenly over the whole month? Why don't they save something for the last week?

It is the kind of question asked over and over with answers that rise out of the subconscious as well as the conscious mind. If you ask Willie Johnson if the children ever leave the table hungry, he replies, *"If they do, they never say nothing."* If you ask the older children, they say, as one did, *"No, not really hungry,"* but if you ask if they would like more to eat they are quick to mention those things they already eat—milk, fried bean cakes, corn bread, chicken, brown gravy. The stomach is a creature of habit and except for the ravening demands of a body close to immediate starvation or one used to well-timed ingestions of good food, it will accept the starchy substitutions without acute alarm and it will, after a time, accommodate its demands to what its owner thinks is normal.

The surge of food the first week of the month and the leanness at the end is common, and to the demand that parents even out the food over the whole month one ends with the reply, "Try it." Try having children go under-nourished for a few days and then when money arrives, try not letting them catch up. Try month after month put-ting some money aside for end-of-the-month meals and having, month after month, some non-food emergency take away that money. When an only pair of shoes disinte-grates or an only pair of trousers is shredded, this is a social emergency, though sharpened by the law that says children must attend school. But food, by instinct, is a life-and-death emergency.

This is one of the many estrangements between the poor and the affluent. Middle-class assumptions of com-mon sense and social responsibility often make no sense to the poor. What is prudent for the well-fed may be irre-sponsible for the poor. For most Americans there is some-thing contemptible in the outlook of the impoverished: don't postpone satisfaction, don't try to save, don't defer pleasure, don't put off until tomorrow any gratification that can be achieved today. For the poor these rules are tried and true. For the poor the future is demonstrably treacherous. Self-denial brings them not the reward of evenly distributed joy but the punishment of permanent loss. When you walk a steady path in life, repeating with comfortable reliability each month's route, it makes sense to leave behind a cache for the moment when, in need, you pass that same spot again. But if you are sliding out of control down the mountain of life or are already at the bottom wandering in the uncharted jungle of desperate daily survival, it is folly to leave anything valuable behind. Prudence, planning, and saving are luxuries of those who possess a surplus and who have confidence in the future.

To this psychological estrangement between the poor and the comfortable is added the differences in common household experiences. This may extend to so basic a habit as the family meal—which some poor never experience as a group—to the more common alienation from those pieces of hardware that are a part of the total American culture. This is the world of the vacuum cleaner, the dial telephone, the bed a child can call his own. The Johnsons have no vacuum cleaner. They have no telephone; the younger children would regard the circular arrangement of numbers and letters as a mystery. The ten Johnsons sleep in four beds. Yet such mechanical fixtures are part of the vocabulary and concepts of the young, and are part of the casual knowledge taken for granted in schoolbooks and intelligence tests. The Johnson children have never seen a movie and since a donated television set broke some time ago have lost even that touch with the outer world.

The sleaziness of much mass culture is justifiably criticized. For the cultural elite it is easily rejected because the family of the aesthete can be without television, movies, or telephones and have richer alternatives at hand—books, conversation, travel. But for the poor, the choice, like that of their bad diets, is television-or-nothing.

Some of the normal elements of life are remembered

by the impoverished parents but even for them the objects and ceremonies of the American culture are receding memories, ever further from their grasp.

"The last picture show I saw," says Mr. Johnson in his habitual recollection of dates, *"was in 19-and-53. It was* The Grapes of Wrath *and* Tobacco Road. *Well, I got a kick out of that* Tobacco Road. *That fellow had a patch on the seat of his pants and he got down on his knees right on the road and prayed to the Lord, asking Him to take care of things, and then this man got up and walked down the road again. Then he turns around and comes back to the same place and kneels down again and says, 'Lord, never mind, I'm going to take matters in my own hands.' I thought that was real funny."*

Did he, Mr. Johnson, ever think of taking things in his own hands?

He looked up with his only trace of bitterness.

"What's there around here for a man to take hold of?"

So, slowly, the poor recede from the customs and ceremonies that bind the rest of society. For the last two Christmases there have been no presents for any of the Johnsons. Nor any tree or household decoration.

"Christmas is the same as any other day. The kids, they talk about it a little, but that's all. Couple of weeks before Christmas the older children said to me, 'Daddy, we don't care for ourselves but we'd like to see something for the little ones.' I told them, 'I just don't have any money.' So Willie, my seventeen-year-old, he hunted and hunted for miles around here for a job to make $3 or $4 to get something for the little ones, but there just isn't a job in the county."

Nor do the children receive any birthday presents. If it is the birthday of the very young there may be some joking at the table for the evening meal. But when the children are in the teens the birthdays pass, usually, without note.

"The last Christmas present I got myself," Willie Johnson said in answer to my question, *"was in 19-and-52. It was a silk shirt, a blue silk shirt, I remember. My wife picked it out."*

He was seated on his porch, his feet on the porch rail. *"I just had to buy myself a pair of shoes seven months ago. Before that, the last pair of shoes I bought was on January 14, 19-and-54. I remember the date because it was on January 30, 19-and-54, on the very same month, that I was cut off from my last job. After that I just wore shoes people give me, neighbors and people like that. The last time I bought a pair of trousers was on February 1, 19-and-59. I had to buy a new pair of pants to go to my mother's funeral. My neighbor let me take a white shirt for the funeral."*

Mrs. Johnson bought a dress six months ago. She is a plump woman, younger than her husband, her brow usually creased with strain and bewilderment. She had walked down the road as we talked and on the porch, by unthinking habit, removed her canvas shoes and walked barefoot in the house. It saves shoes. When did she last buy a dress, before the one six months ago? The brow creased more deeply, the eyes went vague, the shoulders hunched and she smiled apologetically. *"I don't know. It was a long time ago. It was quite a long time ago and right now I can't remember. We just buy when we can. We have to keep those kids in school. But it was quite a long time ago."*

Asked when a doctor was last in the house, Willie

Johnson thought for a moment while he dredged his remarkable recollection of dates.

"There ain't been a doctor in my house since 19-and-51. That was when my little boy went into convulsions. Before then the doc come when three of the babies was caught [delivered] at home. After that the rest was caught in the hospital. Welfare pays for that if it's in the hospital. We use aspirin when they get real sick, else we take them to the hospital."

Life for the children is not dreary. There are railroad tracks and wooded hills and a stream and the unspoiled energy of youth. There are even irrational extravagances like the bottle of Coke or soda each child gets about once a month. They play with marbles. *"They either win or they don't have any."* It is when the mind and the ambitions turn to the larger world that bleakness sets in, even with man's desire to relax. Idleness poisons recreation.

"Recreation? I don't know the meaning of it," said Willie Johnson, who has nothing to do all day long. *"No beer, no whiskey. Don't smoke, don't chew. Don't go to church, though I'm religious. I guess I'm not very strong on churches but I know my Bible and I live by it. She goes to church regular, though."*

Willie Johnson sits on his sagging front porch in a sagging tubed chair and looks out on the steep mountainsides of Logan County. From his green chair he can see the railroad cars of coal shunted by his house daily and he can also see the high ridge on the mountainside where the coal comes from, a strip mine using twenty men and mammoth machines to produce the forty cars he counts each day.

When he was a young man the same amount of coal from a strip mine required five hundred men.

"*Mechanical machinery,*" he said, looking up the mountain, "*is ruining this country.*"

Young Willie sometimes sits on the porch rail and watches the slow-moving shadows of the distant machines. Once he said to his father, "*Daddy, when I grow up there won't be any mines.*" And then, after a long pause, "*Daddy, I wish I could've stayed in school.*"

For the transplanted Scot and Welshman and Irishman in these hills it is not rare to experience a sad pride in departed work, a fierce devotion to family, a quiet doggedness in religion. The only book showing in the Johnson house is a Bible. In the nearby county seat the yellow section of the telephone book lists only twenty-eight surviving coal companies, most of them really in the business of leasing land, but there are 139 clergymen.

Unchurched and religious, Willie Johnson says a prayer every night, a prayer uttered one way or another, in a bitter combination of fervor and fear by millions of parents in Appalachia, in the South, in the shrinking villages and small farms of the United States.

"*Come evening, I'll walk in the back yard and clean it up a bit. After that's done she'll heat some water on the stove and I'll take a bath in the washtub out back. Then I go to bed. At sundown, just like the chickens. Nothing to stay up for. I pray every night. I pray that I'll see another sun go down, pray for just one more day. Then I pray for the same thing I hope for all day. My boy, he wants to be a mechanic and he hopes they'll take him in the Army when he gets old enough. This girl of mine, she's thirteen going on fourteen, and she wants to be a teacher. They talk about this all the time and while they're talking I'm hoping. And every night I pray: they've got to get out of here."*

CHAPTER FIVE

"You know what today is . . . you dumb bastard? Today is Easter!"

"George, you ———head! You know what today is? You know, you dumb bastard? Today is Sunday, April 14. Easter! Easter! And you know what that means? That means a bottla wine is gonna cost you 85 cents, you ———!"

A half-human sound croaked:

"All I got is a ——— seventy cents."

"You ———! Thass what I'm tell' ya. The only way you're gonna get a bottle today is from the bootleggers. There ain't no 50-cent bottles today. There ain't no sales You gotta go to the bootleggers and you gotta pay 'em 85 cents. Don't you know it's Easter, you ———head?"

The animal sound came plaintively again.

"All I got is seventy cents."

"Why, you cheap bastard! You know it's Easter. You got five bucks downstairs advance rent. Go get it, you cheap bastard. Go get it. You know today's Easter and you're too goddam cheap to get your five bucks downstairs, you———!"

From a distant cage a voice groaned.

Nearby someone vomited.

Another voice cried out in sleep.

I went down the long flight of stairs, past the flophouse sign that read, "Clean, Quiet, No Drunks." Outside, a man's motionless body was sprawled across the curb, half in and half out of the gutter.

The Easter sun was just up, pouring yellow, horizontal, and thick down West Madison Street like a searchlight. There was no sound, but moving ghostlike through the blinding light were dozens of men, shuffling, wandering, moving noiselessly in the middle of the street, along the sides of buildings, men who walk all night because they have no place to sleep or who are still standing after a night of wine or have slept in doorways and are in the sun trying to warm muscles gone stiff from sleeping on concrete out of doors. A few purposeful men already rifle the trash barrels for the treasured empty bottles, worth half a cent toward the golden goal of 50 cents, the price of one pint of red fluid marked "California Port," of the lowest possible quality which in brutal quantities dominates foodless bodies to produce the strange narcosis through which some men choose to die slowly, all for 50 cents a pint. Except that this was Easter and the price would be 85 cents.

This was Skid Row in Chicago, a champion in size, but only one of the identifiable neighborhoods in the country's hundred largest cities where men congregate to accompany themselves over the edge of civilized life and then over the edge of life itself.

The derelicts of Skid Row are a common image of the poor: men who live wretched lives because they are mentally or physically sick, who have given up on life or who never tried, whose misery is the debris of the wreckage of human personality.

The winos, panhandlers and muggers of Skid Row

come as close as any of the poor to proving the thesis that poverty follows personal failure. But the wrecks are not typical of the poor. They are a few hundred thousand of the more than 30,000,000 American impoverished. Indeed, they constitute only 60 per cent of Skid Row itself. The first assault upon the visiting eye comes from the derelicts, the bums, the brawlers, the men with busted mouths and bloodstained chins, the bearded barrel dredgers, the winos with the red splotches on the face. But the more one stays on Skid Row the more he begins to notice the neatly dressed men with shaven faces who appear to be at home, quietly circumventing the sprawled body, noncommittally navigating the flow of drunks weaving out of a bar. These are mostly retired bachelors, maybe former seamen or truck-drivers, who can live more cheaply here than anyplace else or who prefer the naked drama of Skid Row to the bore-dom of a placid rooming house in a conventional neighbor-hood. Not a few may live there for whatever sense of su-periority they get from dwelling among the failures, though it must be said that most of the whole men who live in Skid Row view their fragmented neighbors with sadness and pity.

Curiously, Skid Row, along with most of the other urban poor areas, is the beneficiary of the bulldozer and the wrecking ball, which have been compulsively wiping out great chunks of American cities for the last fifteen years. This is a threat to the poor because typically they lose the only homes and neighborhoods they know, wretched as they are, in favor of parking lots, office build-ings, and high-rent apartments, scattering the poor to be-come metastasized seeds of future slums. Nevertheless, the bulldozers have brought some light. During the last generation, welfare work has become professionalized and overwhelmed with more cases than it can properly handle; it has been under primary pressure to save money rather than people, and assumptions made thirty years ago have tended to become perpetuated by ruling committees and workers in the field. Like surgeons, welfare workers have had to inure themselves to suffering, to allocate their attention to the salvageable cases, which usually means the most attractive ones. But the bulldozers are the instrument of a new breed of community tinker, the city planners and redevelopers. They are subject to their own weaknesses; already many of them are more concerned with theory than with people, and it is not unknown that they have their own frozen assumptions. But at least theirs is a fresh eye and they have produced some of the most significant new information on the poor. Among the better redevelopers there has arisen a new spirit of human rehabilitation, taking advantage of the fact that they have excited minds in a new profession, more money than welfare agencies, and the enthusiastic support of the commercial community (unlike the welfare agencies). Since Skid Row is usually the most dramatic social sore and closest to the downtown high-rent district, it has been among the first to come under this bright new eye.

Skid Row, Chicago urban renewers discovered, has most of its men between ages forty-five and fifty-nine, about half of them either on old age pensions or some kind of relief. Almost 90 per cent are white, about two per cent American Indians, the rest Negroes and Puerto Ricans. Most live on incomes ranging between $500 and $1500, though some, of course, have no discernible income at all. The great majority are neither the illiterates nor the derelict Ph.D.s that romantics ascribe to Skid Row, though there are a few of both.

Skid Row Man lives half as long as the average American. The death rate in the thirty-eight cubicle hotels in Chicago is higher than in India, Africa, and the Middle East. The men, typically, die alone and without medical attention. They have 233 times more fatal heart disease than the national average for males, thirty-seven times more tuberculosis, sixteen times more death because of alcoholism, fifteen times more dying from falling down, fourteen times more pneumonia. Sixty per cent of their death certificates are not signed by attending physicians.

My flophouse room was a steel cage, a windowless cubicle with mustard-colored corrugated steel walls. It was eight feet long and not wide enough to stretch the arms wide. It was eight feet high, the top covered by chicken wire, through which came a cable terminating in a naked electric bulb. Inside was a slender steel locker, a broken wooden stool and a cot with one blanket, one sheet, and multitudes of lice. My cage was No. 270 on the third-floor loft, a labyrinth of narrow steel passageways. The stench was solid, sticking in the throat for days after, a mixture of urine, vomit, dirty socks, sweaty bodies, and smells unidentifiable.

One hour before, I had left a room in the Palmer House. On the way to a shower stall at Union Station, while I still had on a conventional business suit, I stopped at a busy orange drink stand and asked the young girl to change a dollar bill. She did and handed me the change

with a pleasant, "Yes, sir." Twenty minutes later I came
back in paint-splotched shoes, old black trousers, khaki
shirt, and ragged sweater, a wrinkled threadbare raincoat,
the part out of my hair, carrying an old brown canvas zip-
per bag. I asked the girl for an orange drink and she served
me, holding the drink until I had put the money on the
counter, her face frozen and hostile and never looking directly at me. I already felt the blank wall between me and
respectable society by which a man can walk as though invisible. If he asks directions he may get no answer, as
though his voice made no sound, or he may get a flash of
fear and revulsion in the eye of the man he asks. It is re-
markably easy to become an emotional exile from one's
own society.

West Madison Street was the usual succession of bars,
used-clothing stores, employment offices ("Pay at the end
of each day"), religious missions, hashhouses, and signs:

CLEAN, INDIVIDUAL ROOMS—NO DRUNKS.

FIREPROOF!

WORKINGMAN'S PALACE HOTEL—ELEVATOR SERVICE, RIDE
UP, DON'T WALK.

FULL SHOT & BEER—25¢.

The place to be on a Saturday night in Chicago's Skid
Row is Rothschild's, a barn of a saloon with great U-shaped
bars and a Klondike atmosphere, festooned with paper signs
proclaiming: FOOT-LONG POLISH SAUSAGE, 27¢ and SHOT—
13¢ and the self-righteous, GET A FULL GLASS OF WINE. It
is well to wait out one's change with care, for eyes note the
drunk who seems to have money and is careless. An elderly
American Indian spoke phrases in Italian, Polish, German,
Greek, Spanish, and Yiddish, made a miniature beer stein

disappear up his sleeve, swallowed flame, and cadged free beers all night with dignity and contempt. If he were asked where he learned Italian he would say, "*You ask too goddam many questions. Do I ask where you came from? Where you spent the last sixty days? I can tell, you're one of those people who's always wanting to know, 'Why?' 'Why?' 'Who-you?' 'Where you from?' Take a tip from me, fellow. Don't ask so goddam many questions and you'll get along better around here.*" Once when the Indian was telling how he overcame a bunch of jackrollers outside a dice game by wrapping hair around his finger and pounding the owner's head against the pavement, my eyes wandered to a fistfight on the other side of the barroom, and the Indian said angrily, "*Hey, don't pay attention to that. You're what I call an eagle eye—always looking, always looking. You better learn it's smarter not to see everything.*" The noisy brawl was extinguished with ease. A bartender nodded his head and two policemen came in, frisked the men, looked inside their caps for knives, and hustled them out.

The bars of Skid Row have strict protocol: anyone attracting the attention of outside reformers is swiftly suppressed. A bearded old man came up to the bar, pitifully held out his palm bearing one penny and said, "*I'm only asking for a couple of pennies to make up a dime,*" and a drinker at the bar snarled,

"*Get the hell out of here. You're not asking, you're begging.*"

Outside it was chilly. There was an all-night movie. "*It's a good place,*" a man in a doorway said. "*It's warm and they let you sleep. But you sleep and got good shoes maybe you wake up and your shoes is gone.*" Inside the "Helping

Hand Gospel Mission" there was a long pink-walled room with a hundred folding chairs and a bored, pot-bellied man in a T-shirt handing out hymn books at the door. A prissy woman in plaid dress and gold-rimmed glasses played the piano. In the front row were eight properly dressed respectable people, plainly the home support for the preacher, while behind them were twenty ragged men, most of them asleep, awaiting the coffee that could be smelled somewhere else in the building for those who paid the price. The price was an endless sermon by a preacher of Scandinavian origin, deep voice, and difficulty pronouncing "th." The monotone filled the room like a narcotic vapor, *"De tree disciples took de Lord into de garden . . ."* and it was possible to wake up later and hear, *"And den der was Sodom and Gomorrah,"* while the ragged men slept on, the coffee odor made stomachs rumble, and it was hard to believe that even the protecting Spirit was not asleep.

Up the street was a narrow, dark bar of the kind which is devoted, usually, to tired B-girls or is a watering place for prostitutes, but inside, after eyes got used to the gloom, there were only three tired men and a huge woman who seemed to be the wife of the bartender. There isn't much sex on Skid Row. It is a place where wine overwhelms even the impulse for women and song.

Inside the flophouse cubicle one could hear a man enter the cage next door. The bottom of the steel walls is perforated with one-inch holes. I never saw the face of my neighbor—we never came and went at the same time—but I could see his high black eyelet shoes which he carefully took off and placed on a newspaper spread on the floor. Then he peeled off brown wool socks. He had an eagle tattoed on each foot. He placed his wooden stool against the door to his cubicle, so that it would fall over if someone forced open the door. Then he put out his light and went to sleep. I put my wooden stool against my door.

The sounds of the flophouse at night came in surges, each breaking through the uneasy narcosis of the others. There were groans, snores, cries, coughing, spitting, gurgling, vomiting, men calling out in Polish, German, and profane English. The doors slammed as the winos left their bottles outside for companions who would wake up in the night, sick.

The sounds in the night are much like those of men dying. The maids who have the unpleasant task of going through the cubicles each noon find on an average one man dead a day in the city's flophouses.

"Oh, Lord," an old man's voice cried out in the night. "Oh, Lord, have mercy on my soul. Oh, Lord, I'm sick. I'm dying. Please, oh, Lord, please have mercy on my soul."

A voice from another cubicle barked, "Shut up, you bastard!"

The old man did not die.

But other men, too, cried out, for only during sleep, with most of them, do the jagged pieces of their former lives float up to the surface, like the cry in the night, "Where's my Dad? Where's my Dad?" and the wild sobbing.

The younger men still sliding down to destruction can sometimes reconstruct some of their past. There was the twenty-nine-year-old man on the West Coast, puffy-faced, his eyes alternatingly searching and vague, his manner uncertain, his sentences always in proper grammar but often dying in the middle or careening off in another direction. His father died when he was seven and his mother remarried a man with two children of his own; they were divorced, and at age thirteen he went to private schools, never again to live regularly at home. He joined the Navy and then the Air Force, washed out of pilot training and quickly descended into Skid Row alcoholism. He had trust funds waiting for him and he learned every ingenious way to extract funds for drinking. He refuses to speak of his mother, but he calls his stepfather now and then.

"I called my stepfather in Frisco and he said, 'I want one thing understood. Under no circumstances are you to come to my home. Now. How are you?'"

He was, as a matter of fact, drying out at the Salvation Army, but the prospects were not good.

"The last month all I can remember eating was two hamburgers. I must have eaten more, but I can't remember it. I can remember vaguely going to St. Anthony's for some beans at lunch. I come here to the Salvation Army for supper when I think I can take the ear-beating about religion."

He remembered selling his blood for wine money. He got $4 a pint. The proceeds went toward a "mickey," a pint of cheap wine for 35 cents, or a "jug" which is a quart for 65 cents, or if he felt unusually prosperous, a brand of real wine for 85 cents, the lower prices reflecting the California source. Winos believe the cheap wine has ether in it, though it does not, according to conventional bottlers.

What impressed him most in his rememberable last episode is that he, the product of private schooling, an expensive military academy, some time at a good college,

possessor of a fairly respectable trust fund in an Eastern
bank, learned how to be a spectacular success as a beggar.

"I was looking thirsty one morning and this old man
gave me a drink. This straightened me out and the old man
said, 'Come on, let's get some dough.' I said, 'How?' and
he said, 'Panhandle.' I said, 'Me?' and he said, 'Sure,
it's easy.' Well, I turned out to be a damned good pan-
handler and I'm not boasting. I'm really good. I have to
be half looped before I can do it but once I get going I
can make enough to support two or three guys drinking,
which is just what I did.

"If I really put my mind to it I can do very well. You
know, hit the businessmen coming out of the good bars.
They come out, they've been drinking and they're feeling
pretty good. I don't give them any baloney. I stay as close
to the truth as possible. That's the trick to really good pan-
handling. I'm in half a blackout all this time, you understand, but if I'm operating well, I can really make money.
The trick is to have some sense of humor. Most panhandlers
aren't very bright about it and the worst thing is they have
no humor.

"I go up to a businessman when he comes out of a bar
and I say, 'Sir, do you have 25 cents? I want a drink.' If
they look like bright guys with a sense of humor, I say, 'Sir,
do you have 50 cents? I want to buy a pint of coffee.' If I'm
really on the high side I'll say, 'Sir, do you have a couple
of bucks? I need a fifth of coffee.' The usual response is,
'Well, at least you're honest,' and they shell out.

"If I get a dollar and I'm not too anxious for a pint of
wine right away, I'll use the buck as an investment. You go
into a pretty good bar and get into conversation with a guy

who looks as though after awhile he might hand you four or five bucks. All you do is listen to him. You'd be surprised how many guys in bars need someone to talk to and if you learn how to listen they'll buy you a lot of liquor. In the last year I didn't earn a single cent at work, but I spent about $100 a month, some of it squeezed out of my trustee with stories, really great stories on why I needed dough, but most of it from panhandling. I can't tell you what I did most of the time but I remember a few things now and then."

The sharing of wine among the winos is traditional and necessary. To be "sick"—suffering from a hangover from cheap wine—is so terrible a condition that it is unheard of for any wino not to share his wine with a sufferer. In the flophouses with cots and steel walls one can hear during the night a noise like a machine-gun, a trembling staccato, the sound of winos in uncontrollable shaking in their cots.

"When a wino is sick, it's like nothing any other kind of drinker has ever known. I know because I was a wino for eight years."

Paul is a perceptive, gentle man of forty whose life fell apart after he left a Jesuit seminary, tumbling from circus roustabout to carnival to Skid Row alcoholism until he hit bottom and now is in a West Coast Salvation Army shelter writing a master's thesis on the lives of derelicts.

"When you're sick you retch with the dry heaves, but, of course, that's the same as an ordinary hangover. Then you get the sweats, then hot and cold flashes that can scare you pretty badly. And then the shakes. Everything in you, in your head and your stomach, your joints, is in pain and

at the same time you're shaking all over. There's nothing you can do to stop it. If you're in a bed, the whole bed shakes. If you press yourself against the wall, the wall shakes. All the time you're sweating as though you have a 105 fever or suddenly you're so cold you cry out in pain, and you're nauseated but you can't throw up any more, and the shakes go on. One or two drinks and all this stops. No alcoholic will ever deny you a drink when you're sick. When I was drinking I could do two fifths of whiskey a day without any food at all, in a stupor most of the time, and then the shakes. By that time you really are pretty sick. I mean physiologically you're in bad shape. And there's no doubt about it. To stay alive, you're sure you've got to have a drink."

Paul is a rare combination of brutal experience, high intelligence, scholarly discipline, and a deep ethical compassion.

"Most of the men on Skid Row come from working-class families. Their fathers probably had unskilled jobs. The men themselves are often looked on as of low intelligence but I'm not sure their range of intelligence is very different from men at large. Don't forget that when they reach Skid Row they've had ten to fifteen years of being beaten by life. They're apathetic and sick and appear stupid. What this comes from, mostly, is that they have, by this time, an extremely narrow outlook—their whole being is directed at food, shelter, wine. At this point there's no question a large proportion of them are mentally defective or ineffective and emotionally disturbed. If they have any ambition left at all, the best job they can get is a terminal one—maintenance worker or hospital clean-up at $40 a week or less and that won't support a satisfactory life. Around here that pays for room and board and nothing else, no laundry, no beer, no clothes, no entertainment.

"There's one trouble with the people who help down here. I have the greatest respect for most of them. The religious people, the Salvation Army, for example. There's no question that their religious feelings bring them here and for that you have to be grateful. But their appeal is a narrow one. There are relatively few men who can accept the kind of special, fundamentalist commitment to religion which is the only salvation they are offered. It's alien to most of the men, especially the ones who are really looking for a way out."

Paul had something to say about the stigma of poverty and failure that follows the man who re-enters working society.

"Remember one thing. Poverty is something everyone hates. The people with money hate it and the people who are poor hate it. The poor hate to be thought of as poor. And people with money hate to look at the poor. I think the worst part of that is the feeling the poor themselves have. When you're poor you walk the streets with the feeling that people are thinking you've got no right to be there, you don't belong, no matter how well-dressed you are. Even now when I leave Skid Row and go to the respectable parts of town I feel the same way. There are little cues you get from respectable people that give you a sense that you aren't part of society. And even without these subtle cues, you have some within yourself. When I go out to meet people—intelligent, understanding people who have jobs and homes and a productive place in the world

—they remind me that for years I goofed up, that I was helped by people like themselves who did the monotonous and responsible jobs that keep society going while I've been failing and not doing my part. That feeling's there even after you've straightened out. Add to that the look in people's eyes when they find out the world you come from, and it can get pretty uncomfortable."

CHAPTER SIX

"I have to admit the machine did a better job than we did."

John Merrick is a 32-year-old American Negro of ordinary appearance—five-feet-five, slender, simple clothes, plain speech—who lives in an undramatic place—Providence, Rhode Island, once the nation's wellspring of religious freedom but now an exhausted textile barony trying to be reborn—and dwells in an uninspiring home—a third-floor flat in a public housing project with the standard yellow hallway tiles, broken door knockers, and cooked cabbage smells.

And yet John Merrick moves with an historic rhythm. He is no fierce fighter of Biblical vengeance or proletarian fire, borne on the tide of noisy battle. Instead he fights in the privacy of his own spirit, among the cabbage smells, on the commonplace battlefields of bureaucracy, against nothing he can see, opposing no one he hates, in a campaign with no beginning or middle or end, for a prize impossible to possess forever. He is merely an American who once had nothing and who tried to make a normal life for his children by doing everything his society says is right, by doing it earnestly and unremittingly.

He has, on the surface, all it takes for a workingman's prosperity. He is a member of a militant union, the United

Steelworkers of America. He has a high-pay industrial craft. There are books in his home. He is an extraordinarily good neighbor. He is active in civic associations. He has shown ambition, pride, responsibility, adaptability, and perseverance. He presses for every hour of work he can get. But he lives poised on the razor's edge between failure and fulfillment. With him is balanced more than that: American society has a graver stake in the fate of all the John Merricks than it, so far, has been willing to recognize. He is Everyman for many millions of contemporary Americans.

The first twenty-four years of John Merrick's life were spent in Zebulon, North Carolina, a backwater village twenty-two miles east of Raleigh. His father was a sharecropper with a family of thirteen, a man who worked the same farm all his life in the familiar, melancholy ritual of the rural South.

They lived in a seven-room ramshackle house with daylight showing through the walls. When it rained everyone got up in the night and stacked the beds in one dry corner and folded the bedclothes in another. For heat there was an open fireplace in the front room and a wood stove in the kitchen. They slept three and four to a bed. On many winter nights they went to bed with their clothes on. They had electricity but water came from a well. They did not have meat very often, except for salt pork. The farm raised cotton, tobacco, and corn, but it was perpetually in debt to the landlord whose demands seemed to rise and fall with the value of the crop. They all had shoes, reserved for church and school, and then using twine for lacings. If clothes money ran out, the oldest schoolchild dropped out to earn enough money to buy shoes so that younger brothers and sisters could continue their education. The exit usually occurred in the ninth grade. John was lucky. He finished the eleventh.

The Merricks maintained a microscopic edge on their family budget until even this margin was wiped out by a distant event: the Korean War and its sudden jump in prices. John was nineteen then and possessed a special insight into this economic phenomenon.

"It was very simple. The major item we bought at the store was flour, because my mother baked all our bread. A 25-pound sack of flour lasted five days in our family. In 1950 the price went up from $6 to $7.50. So we ate less bread."

Already, young John had noticed another socio-economic fact of sharecropping life: the profit his father made on his crops was conversely related to how deeply his father was in debt, and a sharecropper with a family of thirteen was always in debt.

"I remember 1947 was a good tobacco year. And I remember that when everyone found this was going to be a good year for price, the landlord told my father, 'Benny, things are different this year. You've got to pay up all the money you owe me right now.' He knew the price of tobacco was going to be high after the crop was in but he knew my father didn't have the cash to pay his debts until the tobacco was sold. My father had to turn his tobacco over to the landlord ahead of time at the landlord's price and then the landlord made the profit on the high price. I remember telling my father, 'Daddy, there must be another way to live,' and I remember him answering me,

'John, we have no other choice.' I told him, 'Daddy, I prom-
ise you, some day things will change.' "

When John married in 1949 he brought his bride to
live in his father's house. This crowded the household even
more. But John was earning $27 a week cutting timber for
a sawmill and after he and his wife paid their personal expenses and the house electric bill they were able to give
about $15 a week to John's father. By 1951 they had two
sons.

John Merrick made his great decision about racial integration on May 13, 1954, four days before the justices of
the United States Supreme Court made theirs. At 7 o'clock
that morning he showed up at a wooded plot on which the
sawmill had leased cutting rights, but before he could begin
the boss told him, "John, you can't work on this job. The
man who owns this land says he doesn't want any niggers
on his place."

John told the boss:

"Well, I'm here to do a job to support my family. If
you refuse to let me work at my job, pay me off. This is
my last day. We are not animals. We are human beings.
I'm leaving."

John left, but not just the job.

"I left North Carolina because I actually made up my
mind that under the Constitution of the United States of
America this is supposed to be a free country. Why was it
because I am a Negro I couldn't work at a job I'm qualified
to do? I couldn't buy a sandwich in the nearest store? Why
did I have to go to the back door of a restaurant? All these
things sort of came to a head when some white man I never

saw and who never saw me said I had to quit my job because I was a Negro. I realized times were getting modern. I didn't want my children to grow up misled about their rights. I didn't want them to have to live like my father. I didn't want them to have to live like me."

John left North Carolina with $13 and spent $2.88 for a one-way bus ticket to Norfolk, Virginia. There his older brother was a sheetmetal worker with a roofing company. His brother put him up and got him a job with his boss. Two months later John's wife and children joined him in their own flat. They were making $54 a week.

"From $27 a week to $54 sure looked good. And don't let anyone fool you. It wasn't just the country boy looking at a lot of cash. Things really were better. We lived in three big rooms in a place that had a nice yard. Don't forget we had all lived together in one room before. We had never had our own private beds. We had slept in a house where rain came through the roof and soaked the bedclothes, where lots of nights when it was cold we couldn't take our clothes off to sleep. Here I was, 24 years old, and I had my first private bed, my first steak, my first pork chops. We'd raised hogs at home but we always had to sell the chops for cash. The family ate the fat. Now we had meat every day. Corned beef hash. Chops. Hamburger. Steak. Milk. Orange juice. My kids were getting strong. They were actually getting balanced meals.

"Back home when a kid got sick there were home remedies but not much else. Now these kids were healthy because they ate well and they were in a clean house and out of the weather and they saw a doctor who made sure they were growing right. Back home on the farm when a *kid didn't eat right and missed vitamins, he didn't grow right and he could never make it up. It is not a word of lie when I tell you that going from my father's farm in Zebulon to a city job in Norfolk was like going from darkness into light.*"

In Norfolk John met another Negro roofer who had grown up in New England and planned to return because pay was better, housing more attractive, and there was less color prejudice in jobs. The Merricks moved to Providence where his friend's uncle got him a job in a foundry. They lived in a five-room flat that cost $25 a month. Pay went from $54 to $72 a week. But his family was getting larger and he began to feel the vulnerability of the newcomer on the way up.

"*My living was better but my overhead was more. I had to buy tools, brushes, socket wrenches. I was on 30-day trial and I don't mind telling you I was nervous. I used to get headaches from the strain because I was working a $7000 machine I could have ruined. But the other men in the foundry, white and colored, helped me learn and with their help I made it.*"

By late 1958 the Merricks were living in the flickering light of a fluctuating national economy and the growing burden of a family that had grown to nine. There was a recession and the foundry laid off help. John was the last man hired so he was the first to be dropped. He discovered that though city life provides the cash income that buys strong bodies for children it provides no rambling ancestral household that can absorb the temporarily unemployed and no back acre of vegetables to substitute for the visit to the store. In the city when the worker's income goes from

$72 to zero his children's food and their shelter can also go to zero. There were some cushions. The state had unemployment insurance that paid $32 a week, but this would not feed the seven children or pay the rent. The city had a welfare program to supplement unemployment compensation and this added another $38.50.

John kept looking for jobs. He had to turn one down because it was thirty miles away and he had no car. A few months later he found a job as pourer in a foundry at $96 a week. He was back on his own. Fourteen months later all the employees received final notices: the foundry was being demolished in an urban renewal program. The next week John got a job on a moving van at $65 a week, but this was too little to feed the children so welfare added $30.

By then urban renewal had reached his own flat and the landlord, his building condemned, got a court order evicting all the tenants and the Merricks were literally moved onto the sidewalk with their furniture. The head of the local Urban League got the local newspaper to photograph the sidewalk scene, helped move the Merricks back, and dared the landlord to take him to court. From there the Urban League got the Merricks into a public housing project. The brick blockhouses of the project, the steel fence around the laundry lines, the concrete "playyards," the dreary hallways had all the aesthetic blight of the conventional low-income public housing development. But for the low-income family it is still the Promised Land. The law adjusts rent to income, it limits the number of children per bedroom, it makes sure conditions do not drop below given limits of safety. There was no other way the Merricks could have afforded a six-room flat that met minimum standards. Shortly after that he seemed to enter the vocational Promised Land: a $120-a-week job as molder, protected by a strong union, in a big, prosperous firm, the Grinnel Corporation.

For two years life was stable and happy, though by now he had ten children. In 1961 the most modern of blows fell: automation. In April the plant notified the last seventy-five men hired in the foundry that their jobs would be abolished by a new automatic machine. John Merrick describes the collapse of his Promised Land without rancor:

"We were making fittings for bathtubs, radiators, fire hydrants, and industrial piping. In molding you pour metal into one side of a form, then turn the form over and pour the other side. You can make various mistakes that might spoil the work. You can make mistakes that can spoil you, too. If you don't get the molten metal exactly into the opening of the form, you can get bad burns from the splash. I have to admit the machine did a better job than we men did.

"When the Steelworkers Union heard we were going to be laid off they worked out a plan with the company not to lay us off but let us form a labor pool to get first crack at any other work that showed up anywhere in the plant. The union fought for us and the company agreed to do what it could. So we went into the company's labor pool where we did odd jobs as they came up. This is the way it's been ever since. I went from $120 a week to an average of about $75. And $75 isn't enough for ten kids. Some weeks I might work as a sand muddler and get $96. Other weeks I'd do common laboring and get $69. It's pretty hard *to plan your life. We squeezed on everything in the house. But you face a tough problem deciding what to squeeze. You're squeezing the kids, not yourself. And when a man's invested everything he has into a good home, well you hate to give it all up and, well, this is what you spend your life working for."*

He sat in a living room surrounded by signs of middle-class niceties about to crystallize, symbols of comfort and repose, of civilization beyond physical survival, elements of a household that silently and indelibly condition the minds and tastes of children, as well as salve the ego of the parents. The bookcase in the Merrick home is not a high-brow library but it has a dictionary, some book club novels, a nature guide, the Bible, and a home mechanics manual. Inexpensive, conventional art reproductions are on the walls. Shelves and window sills are covered by chinaware figures and small cups and saucers that Mrs. Merrick likes to look at and the girls to play with.

"When things had been good I had bought a TV set, rugs, box springs and mattresses, and a hi-fi set," John Merrick said, looking at his possessions. *"These payments come to about $32 a month. We budget about $45 a week for food, but you know our kids drink twenty-one quarts of milk a week and that comes to $5.50 right there. We ran into all kinds of problems. I wasn't completely unemployed but what pay I got varied from week to week. I had things in my house that a man on welfare isn't supposed to have but if I got rid of them I wouldn't be any better off and maybe worse off. Like that telephone there. I pay $7.88 a month for that. But it makes a difference in my working, especially if I'm on call for pickup jobs.*

"I'm still meeting my monthly payments on almost all of our furniture. If I stopped the payments I'd lose all I'd put into furnishing the house. So we pay out the $45 a week for food, $8.50 on furniture payments, $2 for the telephone, $3.50 a week for the five boys at the Boys Club, and then $15 a week for everything else—clothes, haircuts, everything else for twelve people. But there's still the $59 a month for rent and all this comes to more than my pay. So I get welfare to make up most of this difference. It's a strain though, and it's kind of funny to some people that we live this way and still get the supplementary welfare. We still keep our recreation. Every Saturday I coach a South Providence Little League ball club and my wife plays tennis, free, at Roger Williams Park with the wives of the Boys Club. This doesn't cost money out of your pocket but it's one of those things you don't think of as going with welfare.

"I don't know how long I can go on like this, half hanging on. A father loses face with his kids when he can't provide the things the other kids have. I've always got up for breakfast with the kids even when I'm on a night shift because I want them to know me and I want to know them and I don't want them to think anything is more important to me than they are. So we all know pretty much what the score is. They know things are getting tight, but they've got friends, a healthy life, Boys Club teams. I don't want to take any of that away.

"They still have ambitions, too. One wants to be a machinist. Another wants to be a doctor. One of them wants to be a baseball player. One wants to be an engineer. Kids will change their minds but this isn't crazy or foolish *with them. They have some idea what jobs like that mean and I want them to keep thinking that way. I don't want them to think it's all useless. I don't know the answer. I know the union is honest on this. They're fighting for me and I know it doesn't make any difference that I'm a Negro. But I don't know the answer."*

Uncertain employment and welfare payments have not dampened his spirits. He is active in the Urban League. He studies city politics because he thinks too many low-income citizens ignore self-government. He is vice president of a neighborhood self-help league that is mostly Negro. When a neighbor was burned out of his house, the Merricks took in the family of six for a month. *"We slept on floors, sofas, everywhere. But what else could the man do?"* When John discovered that one of his children's playmates was desperately hungry he found the father was like himself—big family with twelve children, low pay as a chicken-plucker at $55 a week, supplementary welfare—but he was sinking into alcoholism. John paid him a visit.

"I could get the truth where a social worker couldn't. I knew his wife wouldn't complain to the welfare about his taking money to drink instead of feeding the kids because that's a serious welfare offense and they'd demand their money back and attach his pay to get it. I told him he needed a better job. He said he couldn't get a better one because he's a Negro. I told him, 'Joe, you were a welder and a bulldozer operator in the Navy. Your skin was black then, too. Don't go using your color as an excuse.' I know his skin made a difference. Those construction trades are tough for a Negro to break into. But it isn't just color. It's tough for the Irish and Poles, too. They say you have to

be Italian. But you can't just sit and complain. Well, to make a long story short, Joe's making $93 a week now in construction and his welfare's been cut 'way down. He's stopped drinking. I could talk to him because I'm in the same boat. He knows I know what I'm talking about. He knows he can't fool me with a lot of excuses."

The Merricks are having trouble and they are poor, basically because the industry he is in, and the economy it operates in, is not active enough to nourish all its new urban citizens. But he is poor, too, because his family is so large.

"The main problem with us has been that while our income went up, our family got bigger, so big that my income just couldn't keep up with it. If I didn't have such a big family it would be easier to get over these rough spots. We didn't know anything about birth control. If the American Negro had known about birth control thirty years ago things would be a lot different today."

It is not just the American Negro who specializes in large families and low incomes. It is common among all rural families. The hard limitations of the city apartment and the precise mathematics of dividing people and groceries comes too late to country families grown in a rambling house surrounded by space and food and for whom education, nutrition, and medicine are disposable luxuries. But John Merrick insists that innocence plays its part.

"Don't take for granted that everyone grows up knowing about birth control. Maybe city boys do. But country boys don't. Not the same way, not as much as in the city. There just isn't the same kind of experience and contact with people who really know about these things. You may

not believe it, but my wife and I didn't know you could get good medical advice on birth control until 1959. We didn't know that doctors could help, or that there are clinics for this. It's a big secret that a lot of welfare people won't talk about. We had our eighth child before we found out about proper birth control. My wife was tired, it was wearing her down taking care of all the kids. So we asked our doctor and he said that if a woman's health would be jeopardized by getting pregnant then there were certain steps that could be taken, but if a woman is healthy it's very difficult to do anything. The doctor's a Catholic and I suppose that made the difference. One day I was eating lunch with another fellow at work and I told him how I had just had my eighth baby and how hard it was going to be on my wife. And this fellow, he was Italian, said, 'John, what are you talking about? I've been married four years and I've only got two kids.' He was the one who told me how to control the size of our family without being unnatural. It was a little embarrassing and hard to get details, so he said, 'Look, I'll have my wife go over and talk to your wife.'"

That is how—after their eighth child in ten years—the Merricks learned about limiting families. Since then they have been to a privately-supported birth control clinic.

John Merrick had come a long way from the undernourished farm boy helping his father chop cotton, looking down the long rows to see only grinding poverty and the oppression his father and his grandfather had known. His father had told him, *"John, we have no other choice."* But John is a member of a generation, white and black, that made its own choice, that left the permanent depression of the farms and moved to the cities, moved because they need the cities and because the cities, despite their stumbling, need them. In his search for fulfillment, John Merrick turned to Providence, a particular city that took its name from a concept that all cities in this era have become: a refuge for those who can no longer be nourished where they are. But if the cities are providential havens, they are still filled with uncertainty and travail. If they offer salvation, they also have terrible pitfalls.

CHAPTER SEVEN

"I have these debts
I never had before. Never."

The farmer has always been the folk image of The Perfect American: hard-working, self-reliant, his own boss, prospering from his own labor and beholden to no man.

It is an image promulgated by well-fed orators, not just for farmers but for urban Americans as well. They preach the gospel that given his bare hands there is no excuse for a man of character to fail, because each man is master of his own economic fate. Since it is the individual alone who determines his own success or failure, government and society have no responsibility for what happens to a man's livelihood except to let nature take its course. This particular myth is believed most fervently by its hero, the small farmer, which makes all the more poignant his contemporary tragedy.

Farmers and farm workers are among the poorest people in the United States. They aren't very healthy. They do not prosper. And they are so beholden to others that they are among the most desperately debt-ridden citizens in the land.

The fallacy that the Good American has total control over his own income is disbelieved by the industrial worker and small businessman who see that while hard work, thrift, and skill are important they can be swept away by impersonal forces of technology and economics. Yet it seems to come as a terrible shock to farmers that they, like the factory worker, are caught in social change over which they have little influence.

The brutal fact is that most farmers aren't really needed any more. The classic figure, the man with the plow, is still a hero in political oratory but in cold economics he is ridiculous. Forty acres and a mule no longer will support a family. It takes at least 325 acres for an average American standard of living, plus good credit at the bank and heavy investment in fertilizers, weed killers and complicated machinery. Fifty years ago one farmer grew enough food and fibre for seven people; today he provides for twenty-four. There are 312,000 big farms in the United States that produce half of all agricultural sales. The 1,600,000 at the poor end, each earning less than $1000 a year, produce only 5 per cent of sales. At this moment there are over 1,500,000 young men between the ages of ten and nineteen growing up on farms but in the next ten years there will be only 150,000 openings for farm operators. It is a chilling thing when a basic activity of man has room for only one in ten of its children. It is not surprising that in the last ten years 8,000,000 Americans left farms for the cities. By 1973 another 10,000,000 will have left. This has been a revolution come not with trumpet call or clap of doom, but by silent, relentless change that puzzles rather than shocks. Against it most farmers still resist with the compulsive instinct to make things grow and a continuing bitter love for the land.

Columbus Cooper is fifty-seven years old. He inherited his land from his father and cleared it by his own hand, starting when he was sixteen years old. He built his house himself. Four years ago, for the first time, he had to mortgage his home and farm.

On a rainy spring day he stood on the porch of his unpainted clapboard cottage, a rough hand grasping the slender-smooth weather-bleached pine trunk that supported the porch roof. He looked out on his land in Sumter County, South Carolina, at the dull enameled sky, the sagging tobacco shed, the drizzle glistening on the small tractor and moistening the rust on his six-year-old Ford under the big magnolia tree. For him, too, the revolution was a perpetual puzzle.

"Things are kind of standing still. That's what's worrying me. I'd like to redeem myself, but the expenses are growing. Things could break bad for me if I can't stop this expense and pay back my indebtedness. And if the older boys go off on their own, I don't think I could do it all by myself. I'm getting old now."

It is generally agreed that a farmer in the United States, if he wants to live at an ordinary standard of living, needs to gross at least $10,000 a year cash income. Columbus Cooper, with a family of twelve, grosses $1500.

He is no rarity in American farming. There are 350,000 fulltime family farms that average $438 a year in sales. Because he is a Negro, Columbus Cooper is worse off than most. Over 40 per cent of all Negroes in rural areas have less than $1000 a year income. The average white-operated commercial farm in the South has 382 acres, the Negro, fifty-six acres (Cooper has twenty-six acres of his own plus fifteen he rents). The gap between Negro and white farmer increases constantly. In 1950 the median income of colored farm families was 52 per cent of white Southern farm families; in 1960 it had dropped to 45 per cent. Most Southern farm counties are eligible for Federal agricultural aid because of their impoverished Negroes, but most of the aid goes to white families. In nine counties around Cooper's where Negro farmers are a majority, only one of the county committees that decide whether a farmer will get a Farmers Home Administration government loan has a Negro on it. A friend of Cooper's who had farmed twenty-one years and had good credit with the Federal government was turned down by such a county committee and immediately thereafter one of the white members of the committee offered him $10,000 for his 100 acres. Cooper's friend had to borrow $5400 at 25 per cent interest to keep his farm.

Yet white farmers are not much better off. Half earn less than $3000 a year and 20 per cent less than $1000. All farmers are feeling the crush and, while it is easier if one is white, the worst circumstance is to be a *small* farmer, white or black. In 1950 there were 139,000 farms in South Carolina; today there are fewer than 75,000. Against this the Coopers struggle with courage.

Mr. Cooper, a thoughtful man who dresses neatly and looks out steadily through shell-rimmed glasses, can't quote national statistics. But he feels the revolution. "*I built this house myself forty years ago and I had no mortgage on it until four years ago.*" His $2000 mortgage is at 7 per cent, lucky and low for a small farmer. "*I don't get to pay as much on the principal as I'd like,*" he says, but he has reduced it to $1500, some of it with bales of cotton.

But each year he seems to have less cash to start the next crop and has to borrow for seed, fertilizer, and fuel to cure his tobacco.

He is not ignorant of the economics of size. His gross income is $1500 a year, $800 of it from his official allocation of 0.81 of an acre of tobacco and $700 from his allocation of 4.7 acres of cotton. He knows he needs to enlarge his operation to enlarge his income. He applied for an FHA loan to clear twenty more acres for planting, which would bring in perhaps two or three times his present income. But the all-white committee turned him down. This does not necessarily reflect race. There is a decent relationship between the Cooper farm and white businessmen. But Cooper sees what this means in the years to come: as the government reduces acreage to prevent surpluses from the growing yields per acre, all farms are cut proportionately. The farm operator who grosses $100,000 from his tobacco and cotton acreage is cut the same percentage as Mr. Cooper with his 0.81 of an acre of tobacco and his 4.7 of cotton. The big farmer can survive on a cut of 10 per cent in his acreage; Columbus Cooper can't stand a cut of 10 per cent in his $1500 yearly income. Of course, should he and others like him go out of business, their acreage then becomes divided proportionately among the survivors, and many small farmers wonder whether big operators on county committees turn down loan applications with that in mind.

How do you support a family of twelve on $1500 a year?

He grows most of the vegetables they eat—cabbage, collards, turnips, peas, beans. He raises his own pork, selling the better cuts and keeping the fatty ones. If the cow is milking, the children get milk. In summer he and the boys may catch pike and bream and catfish. In winter and fall they hunt for squirrel which Mrs. Cooper boils and then fries. Or they may catch raccoon which she boils and hashes with onions.

They spend about $600 a year for store food—rice, flour, sugar, and occasionally stew meat. He pays $400 a year on his tractor, $200 for fertilizer, $150 for clothes, $85 for kerosene to cure his tobacco, and $200 for life insurance. This provides nothing for the $300 he still owes on his car, nothing on the mortgage, and no provision for medical or dental bills. And it already adds up to more than $1500. The slight additions to the $1500 income are contributions made by the older boys when they get an occasional odd job in the summer, or the sale of pork, or a gift now and then from his eldest son working in the North. The surplus does not go over $200 in the best of years.

Mrs. Cooper is fifteen years younger than her husband but her round, pleasant face looks sad and tired. She thinks she works harder than her mother did. For years both husband and wife have promised themselves they would pipe water into the six-room house but now they speak of the pump in the back yard with weary resignation. They both get up at 5 a.m. and go to bed about 10 in the evening. The youngest child is one year old, the oldest at home is nineteen. The girls' ages are three, five, seven, eleven, and fifteen. "I do a lot of mending and altering hand-me-downs," Mrs. Cooper said and then with eyes closed added, "but they're getting on to their teens and *you know girls that age in school and what they feel about clothes."*

The living room was neat (*"the roof leaks in two or three places but not bad"*), with clean yellow curtains on the windows, an old scrubbed yellow-and-orange linoleum on the floor, two sofas used for sleeping in the summer (there are seven beds for twelve people), and a piano with instruction books on the rack.

"Jo Earl, she's fifteen, takes lessons. They cost 60 cents a week. It's quite a lot for us, but I think the girls ought to have something like that," Mr. Cooper said.

An aunt in North Carolina gave them the piano. Five years ago an uncle in Miami gave them an old TV set. They have a deep freezer they paid $300 for when they got the mortgage money four years ago, using it to preserve summer food. Their farm vegetables, hunting, fishing, and the deep freezer give them a better diet than most $1500-a-year families (and this diet an imponderable support for their obvious strength of spirit).

Their breakfasts include bacon and eggs, "bacon," of course, meaning "soft" bacon or fatback. At noon there are boiled vegetables. For supper there are vegetables, two or three times a week some chicken, canned peaches, or pears in homemade cane syrup, and, if the cow is lactating, milk for the children.

The children's clothing comes partly from the family income, partly from the boys' odd jobs in summer on other farms. Mrs. Cooper bought a dress two years ago. Mr. Cooper bought a suit four years ago. They have not been to a movie since they were married.

Doctors and dentists are visited in desperation.

Though seven of the children are less than nine years old, a doctor was last in the house four years ago when an older boy had pneumonia. When toothaches become unbearable a child visits a dentist in town at $3 a visit. It has worked out to about one visit to the dentist a year for some member of the family. Some of the children have never been in a dentist's office and at the rate so far the probabilities are for one visit every twelve years for each child.

Christmas is still an important day for the Coopers and the parents try to spend $2 per child, getting dolls for the girls and a toy for each young boy. Birthdays are observed, but not with presents. *"We always do something special on a birthday,"* Mrs. Cooper said, *"like have chicken or a sweetbread for supper."*

Though they operate on the lowest income-per-healthy-person imaginable in the United States (less than $2.50 each a week) the Coopers have a strong sense of family, of ambition, and of productivity. Mr. Cooper finished the tenth grade; Mrs. Cooper the ninth. Their oldest son finished the twelfth grade and wanted to go further, but could not because the younger children were in school. A nineteen-year-old boy finished high school and a seventeen-year-old plans to graduate.

One reason for this remarkable family cohesion is, obviously, the strong character of Mr. Cooper and the gentle perseverance of his wife. Another is the persistence of older values of affluence while their family economy gradually deteriorates, though "affluence" is not a good description of the high point of the Cooper fortunes.

"The most I ever made in a year was $2000 in 1947-48," Mr. Cooper said with evident nostalgia. *"But I didn't have*

the headaches and overhead I have now. Right now if every-thing turned out the best it possibly could I might make $2000 a year but I wouldn't be anywhere near so well off as I was back in '48."

One reason $2000 now would be less comforting than fifteen years ago is the increased cost of living and farming. Another is that in the lean intervening years, Mr. Cooper acquired debts which now soak up some of every dollar. But the main reason is that in 1948 he had only three chil-dren and the five Coopers each had $400 to spend that year; if they had the same gross income, the twelve Coo-pers would have only $167 each.

"Only time I used to do pretty good farming I didn't have all the children. I'm standing still but the expenses are growing. I hope when my children go on their own they won't have as big a family as I have. But that's in the Lord's hands, not ours."

The assignment of family size to the Deity is common among the poor, especially the rural, Bible-belt poor, but whatever its cause it is the explanation for the continuing tide to the cities. Millions have left the South and the farms for the cities but the balance between numbers of people and the ability of the land to support them has not been struck, partly because large rural families are repopu-lating the farms.

Mr. Cooper does not complain. He looks steadily at his plight and recognizes it.

"I used to farm with mules but they could up and die in the middle of the season. I'm lots better off with my trac-tor because it does more work than the mule and operating expenses aren't as bad. A good mule would cost $275, $300.

But of course a tractor costs maybe $1200. That's the worst of it. I know I'm better off with the tractor and with the modern fertilizer and seed. But no matter how much better they are, they cost a lot of money and sometimes I can't sleep nights trying to solve my problems.

"I have these debts I never had before. Never. In forty years of farming. The worst one is that $1500 still on the farm, but I farmed thirty-six years before I had to have a mortgage. Right now I got to worry about the $85, $100 for fuel to cook the tobacco. Miz Cooper says the worst months are August for school clothes and December and Easter, but I have my own. It's April. April you've got to start the year with the farm, credit for fertilizer, credit for seed, credit for fuel. I used to pay cash for these things but now it seems I have to have credit. But if you don't solve that April money trouble, you're dead for the year."

Mr. Cooper longs for the ability to pay cash instead of going into debt. He wishes he could get his government loan to clear twenty more acres. He wishes he could be a little bit ahead instead of falling ever further behind.

He was the kind of man an official spoke of in Washington:

"Down on our small farms we've got a hard core of people who are occupationally set in their life pattern. They may or may not have low I.Q. but they possess enough native shrewdness to operate well in their native environment except that they are now shocked and dulled by the loss of their jobs or debts on their farms. There is very little hope for them. I hate to say this, but we've got just so much money to work with in our programs and if we have to decide where to spend it, then we are going to spend it on the *young people. We're just not going to be able to do much with the older folk. But maybe we can catch the young people before it is too late and discouragement becomes permanent and we have a whole generation of lifetime welfare cases."*

Mr. Cooper has ideas about his children, too.

"Mostly I hope my kids do better than I'm doing. They'll have to achieve something on their own and they'll have to study for that, learn modern farming, or a trade like brickmasonry. Everyone can't do farming. But I hope they won't have to leave home. Oh, I hope they won't. But I want them to do better than I have. I'm thankful to be living, to be healthy, and to be able to do the best in me. But I'm not happy enough of the time. I'm not happy now."

The Coopers are in the best tradition of the small American farmer—they are hard-working, sober, courageous, and a fine family. But they are poor, they are getting poorer, and their best hopes are doomed.

As we drove through the spring rain, through the splashing roads that parted the fertile fields, an expert on farming in South Carolina looked out over the land and the lowering sky and said, *"In ten or fifteen years there'll be no small farms to speak of in South Carolina . . . the farmers are going to go to the cities, most of them, or else they're going to starve."*

CHAPTER EIGHT

"I ain't had a letter in twelve months. And that was from the bank."

Edmund MacIntosh was depending on the theory that hard-boiled eggs and opened cans of Spam need no refrigeration. And he was sick.

He had also depended on the theory that if you work hard, live frugally, and mind your own business, you'll get by without help. And now he was seventy-four years old and needed help.

Mr. MacIntosh depended on hard-boiled eggs because his hotel room has no refrigerator and he can't afford to eat out. He is trying to live on his $50-a-month Social Security check. Room rent is $38.50 a month, which provides a room with clean linen every two weeks and clean towels every day. The remainder goes for food and chewing tobacco. Every week friends on the same floor buy him two dozen eggs, seven small cans of V-8 juice, two cans of Spam, a carton of dry cereal (because the box says, "Minimum daily requirement of vitamins") and his tobacco. He boils his eggs at once and eats them morning and evening. He stretches a can of Spam for three days or so. It has cost him violent nausea to discover that hard-boiled eggs and opened Spam need refrigeration in warm weather.

He was trying to eat on $11.50 a month, or 38 cents a

day. The Department of Agriculture thinks that the clever-
est shopper for the minimum needs of an old man has to
have a dollar a day.

It came as almost as shattering a blow that his other
theory about self-reliance also has flaws. He has worked
hard in his time, lived frugally, minded his own business,
but somehow at age seventy-four this has not been enough.
He is slowly starving to death, hastening the invasion of
age.

"*What I need is medical attention*," he says. But he
needs more than that. And so do about 8,000,000 other
Americans over sixty-five who are impoverished. Mr. Mac-
Intosh is not unique. He lives on about $600 a year. There
are 1,500,000 lone individuals in the United States who
live on less than $500 a year. The 8,000,000 aged poor
are a growing segment of the American population who
feel in their bones that they are no longer needed or
wanted. In some primitive societies the old and sick are
placed in a special shelter where they slowly and discreetly
die. In the United States there are no such deliberate
dwellings for death but there are the acres of crumbling
rooming houses and cheap hotels in every city where the
aged await the end. There used to be 3000 old people on
Los Angeles' Bunker Hill alone, and 16,000 inhabitants over
sixty in Uptown of Chicago. Every city has districts where
the aged sit or lie all day, seldom getting outdoors, eking
out a Social Security check or a pension or dwindling savings, but unknown to most of the city. They are known to
the Social Security office, which recognizes the cluster of
addresses in its card files, or the welfare department, or
the Fire Department, which usually has special plans when

an alarm flushes the terrified residents out of the geriatric warrens.

When Edmund MacIntosh was a boy there were fewer than 4,000,000 Americans over sixty-five, only one in twenty citizens. At that time a child at birth could expect to live forty-seven years. For those who cheated this statistic by living longer, the usual fate was to remain a part of a large household in a large house, with children and grandchildren, in the towns and villages of the turn of the century.

Today there are 16,000,000 Americans over sixty-five, one in every eleven citizens. At birth today a child can expect to live seventy years. Four million of the aged live alone, and millions more as couples by themselves, far from their children who live in small city apartments or in compact suburban cottages.

Science is keeping people alive longer. But it is taking away their jobs sooner. In 1920 over 30 per cent of the aged were working. Today only 20 per cent have jobs. The simple jobs that used to be the special preserve of the aged are among the first eliminated by automation. It is impolite to call anyone "old" but this is cruel semantics. Socially, even physically, the extended vigor of Americans make it natural that these be euphemized as "senior citizens" or the "ageing," or, at worst, "the elderly." But when it comes to work, they are old. Today if a man loses his regular job at age forty-five, the odds that he will never find another steady job are frighteningly high. Medical science has made spectacular gains in keeping human beings alive, but social policy has failed to find a civilized way for them to nourish their surviving bodies and spirits. Survival has its price, in high medical costs, in loneliness, and in uselessness. Yet little is done to fill the lengthening empty years. The Department of Health, Education and Welfare says that by the year 2000 there will be 30,000-000 Americans over sixty-five, double the number today. Dr. Herbert S. Robb, of the Wayne College of Medicine, says, *"If we could cure arteriosclerosis, the ordinary life-span except for cancer might be 120 to 130 years."*

A lot of old Americans will recognize the world of Edmund MacIntosh. He has a solid, dignified manner, even as he lies on his bed, propped on an elbow, his square-jawed face turning ashen. His third-floor room in a Los Angeles hotel is painted a vague green. Torn curtains at the window are tied in a knot to let in some light and provide a view of an eroding dirt hillside and the side of a concrete bridge.

He was born in North Carolina, was graduated from high school, finished two years of a military institute. During World War I, in the Merchant Marine, he married a girl from Georgia. They had a daughter. The MacIntosh life was never luxurious but he seemed to earn money adequately. After the first war, he bought a newsstand in Times Square for $200 and cleared $2500 a year from it. When the Depression shrank that income below tolerable limits he went to work in a Baltimore hospital and finally to Washington, D. C. where he worked in a newspaper distributing office and made $3000 a year. This was not enough to keep the whole family together happily and his wife and daughter went to live with one of his relatives while he worked things out in Washington. The day after

Pearl Harbor, Mr. MacIntosh, then fifty-two, volunteered and because of his World War I experience was shipped out as a merchant seaman. He saw his wife before he left.

"*I kissed her goodby when I left and gave her a hug and went. I was in Midway when I noticed the letters was coming farther and farther apart. First they was once a week, then every two weeks, then once a month. I was on a ship when it finally came. I wasn't surprised. It was a notice she was filing for divorce. I read it once and tore it up into little pieces and dropped the pieces over the side. That was that.*"

After the war Edmund MacIntosh went it alone, working steadily and minding his own business. After his discharge he became a civilian guard at an Oakland air base at $38 a week, room free. He left that to become a railroad guard on the Southern Pacific at $80 a week, the high point of his working career.

"*Ah, those were the best days. The pay was good. The work was good. I was doing what I liked. I had friends and saw shows. I was living in a San Francisco rooming house where railroad men stayed, for a dollar a day. Then in '54 the railroad started laying off men. I came down here to Los Angeles after that. It's warmer and it's supposed to be cheaper living.*"

He went from his pleasant railroadman's rooming house to a Los Angeles flophouse at 60 cents a night. He did odd jobs. By now he was sixty-four and nobody wanted to put him on a regular payroll. Mostly he cut lawns in Los Angeles, and cleaned cellars and garages. He lived on $1.50 a day. "*I could get a good breakfast, eggs and bacon, for half a dollar, I'd have no lunch, and a snack for supper, you know, eggs or a hot dog. I was getting by. I had enough to see a picture show once a week."*

Then, about a year ago, after almost ten years as the old man who always came around cutting lawns, automation hit Edmund MacIntosh. He was made obsolete by power lawn mowers.

"They was using more and more of them. I couldn't afford one and when I used the people's mower it took only half the time as with a hand mower and by and by my people realized that, hell, they might as well do it themselves. I don't blame them. With a power mower it's no work at all. But I just wasn't getting enough work to stay alive. That's when I went to the Social Security people. I knew I had Social Security coming to me when I reached sixty-five but I was getting along cutting grass so I went to the Social Security people and asked them if I'd lose anything by not taking it right then. They told me no, it would just pile up, so I let it. But when those power mowers came in and I wasn't making enough to eat, I went to the Social Security people. I didn't mind doing that. Now, welfare, that's charity and that's something else. But Social Security, that's yours, you work for that yourself.

"So last year I went to the Social Security. They was awfully nice and I picked up my back pay and started my $50 a month. I try living on the $50 but it just doesn't work. Some months it's all right, some months it's not. I hate to use all my money in the bank from my Social Security saving because it's all I've got. But now I need help."

Mr. MacIntosh was lucky. Only because he was over 72 did his uncollected Social Security pension accumulate. He

was also lucky he could steadily withdraw money from this
nest egg to augment his monthly payments.

He spit some tobacco from his reclining position. He
didn't quite make it to the green plastic wastebasket on
the floor.

"Well, they've told me about welfare and I didn't
much like the idea of that. But I've done about everything
I can to cut out my outgo. I moved to a cheaper hotel here
and now they're going to tear this one down. I sold my TV
for $15.50 and I miss it now. Maybe I'll have to go to wel-
fare. But I don't know where to go and I'm not able to go
out any more. If I try walking my head swims and I'm
afraid if I go outside I'll fall down and the cops will think
I'm a wino.

"This is a tough neighborhood. I had a friend, older
man like myself, good fellow, didn't drink. He had dizzy
spells now and then and one day he had a spell and stopped
to lean against a lamppost. Well, the cops picked him up
for a drunk. You get one telephone call when they pick
you up and I was the only man he knew so he called me.
He said he needed $21 to make bail but $21 was more than
I had or could put my hands on. He spent thirty days in
jail. So I've been afraid to try walking much outdoors.

"The last time I left this city was seven years ago. Last
time I left this block was two weeks ago. I took a cab to
Third and Main for a haircut that cost me 50 cents. Cab
cost 85 cents. I get my hair cut at the barber school. But
they don't seem to have no taxi school for a cheap ride."

Sometimes in the evening, Edmund MacIntosh will
walk to the elevator on his floor and ride down to the
"lobby" of his hotel, a corridor of depression where ashen

old men sit in torn plush sofas beside a row of orange steel barrels marked "Scrap."

Most of the time he lies on his bed, listening to a cracked plastic radio, mostly to news and discussion programs.

"I like the radio, though I miss my TV. I don't have the money to buy a newspaper. The janitor here's a nice fellow and he brings me an old one now and then. On the radio I like to hear political talks. Best thing I like is the President's press conference. I'm a Democrat in politics. My Daddy was and my granddaddy was. We believed all Republicans go to hell when they die and I didn't want to go to hell. I voted last year for Governor Brown and Mayor Yorty. I voted for Kennedy. I've voted all my life ever since I was old enough. Fact is, I was accused once of voting before I was old enough. I was nineteen years old, pretty near old enough."

He fears the day when even his walking to the elevator will stop and the time when he will not have kind friends. As it is, a couple on the floor look in on him every day. The janitor brings him old papers. Another man does his shopping every week. But the hotel will be torn down and Edmund MacIntosh will be moved among strangers.

"What I need most is a doctor. But I don't know no doctor I can call. I need something for my eyes. Four years ago I went to the hospital and they scraped them and I could read a newspaper without glasses. Now if I shut my right eye I can't see that doorknob over there. My hearing's going, too."

I asked him what things he missed most, now that he is alone in his hotel room. He pulled with his arm against the steel rod of his headboard and let himself look out the window at the bare earth hill and the grey concrete that made his view of the world.

"Things I miss? You haven't got enough paper."

He was silent for awhile. He was good-natured and matter-of-fact.

"My eyes are getting dimmer. I keep having these dizzy spells. I keep getting sick to my stomach. There's not a thing on my stomach right now. I guess what I want more than anything else is a doctor. Some good medicine."

He paused some more.

"I'd like to go to church. I went a year ago but I don't know if I'll be able to go again. I can't right now and it's a little hard for me to tell when I will again. If I will again. Straight up, that is. I need a suit of clothes. I'd love to go to a picture show. That may sound like asking for everything in sight, but I miss things like that."

He chewed some more and spit again. He missed again.

"All right. A man ain't going to have everything all his life. Sure, I'd like to be able to walk around without getting dizzy. And go to church. And go to a picture show. But maybe if I just had some good company I guess that would be all right, too. I ain't had a letter in twelve months. And that was from the bank about my account."

The man referred to in this chapter as "Edmund MacIntosh" died three months after this interview. The coroner's report said death was from "apparent natural causes."

CHAPTER NINE

"I don't want to go up that road any more."

"*Do you know from your own personal knowledge that a hospital refused to take in a man who was dying?*"

William Bell, the Protestant missionary, looked at me blankly.

"*Do I know? I personally drove him to two hospitals who refused him and after driving around most of the night I found a third who finally took him in. When I got home they were on the phone for the patient's background. I said, 'I don't know his background. Why don't you ask him?' and they said, 'Oh, he's dead.'*"

Does he know for a fact that doctors won't come when a child is seriously ill and a fee is vouched for?

"*Our own missionary here called the doctors in town and couldn't find one who'd come out. He went back to the shack where the other kids were sleeping on the floor in burlap bags. And he was holding the baby in his arms when the baby died.*"

"Those who labor in the earth," wrote Thomas Jefferson, "are the chosen people of God."

Jefferson didn't know the American migrant workers, the two or three million men, women, and children who work for pay on other people's farms. Most of them move like nomads from farm to farm, about 500,000 from state to state. They live in the worst squalor, the most hopeless family chaos, and the most ignored poverty of the American poor. They are almost outside the normal workings of American society—except that their hands pick the nation's lettuce, tomatoes, beans, strawberries, onions, potatoes . . .

They are the most interstate workers in the country but they are exempt from Federal minimum wage laws for workers in interstate commerce. Many states don't even require their children to go to school. They are almost never eligible for welfare since they don't live long enough in one place. They can't vote, don't get unemployment compensation when they are out of work, and their families do not get workmen's compensation when they are killed or injured on the job.

Conservative farm organizations like the American Farm Bureau Federation, speaking for the richer farmers, insist there are clean, decent migrant working conditions: there are, here and there. Religious and labor groups and a rare voice in Congress, like Senator Harrison Williams of New Jersey, speak, hardly noticeably, to the more pertinent fact: the massive misery of the great majority of the migrants.

In 1960 the average migrant worker earned $1016. Where there are families the young frequently work. It is hard to get anyone to admit that such a thing as child labor exists, but in 1959 a special U.S. census showed 457,-000 children between the ages of ten and fifteen employed in agriculture. A California study showed 20 per cent of farm injuries were to children under sixteen who were working for pay at the time. Nearly all these families are either Negroes or Spanish-speaking Americans from Texas and California. Typical educational achievement for adults is fourth grade. At least 10 per cent are children under ten.

Theirs is a strange existence. Their seasonal migrations are charted by agriculturists on maps, like those put out by the Audubon Society for birds. But more is known about the birds than about these human beings. On the maps three great routes for the migrant workers spray northward: from Southern California up the West Coast, from Florida up the East Coast, and the greatest movement of all, from Southern Texas fanning outward to twenty-eight other states. About half of these workers are recruited and scheduled by the Federal government to work particular farms for specific crops. About 35 per cent wander on their own with personal knowledge and labor market grapevine intelligence on when and where crops will be ready. And 15 per cent are recruited by private agents hired by big farmers to scout the winter camps in Texas and Florida to sign up workers, usually at $3 a head for the recruiter. Shifting in and out of this pool of migrating humanity, varying according to the success of the big farmers to get permissive legislation in Congress, are a few hundred thousand Mexican workers who enter the United States for a particular season, preferred by the growers because they are generally more stable and predictable and because the migrants' wages, desperately inadequate for an American, are attractive for men whose families live in Mexico.

When the workers move, they travel in old school buses provided by labor contractors, or in the back of trucks or now and then in a family jalopy with an outsider paying a few dollars to go along. They own permanently only what they can carry with them. They live in shacks provided by the farmer. Life is primitive, descending easily into alcoholism and destruction of family.

If you drive north from Miami on Route 441, through a succession of garish growths of neon, to the thirty-five miles beyond Fort Lauderdale, you will see along the road mostly flat, grassy savannas with scarcely a hint that slightly beyond the highway is a world of 35,000 migrant workers—most American Negroes, some Jamaicans and Puerto Ricans, a few whites—living in clusters of shacks, working in the nearby Florida fields for eight months and moving northward for summer crops as far away as Michigan and Maine, but focusing mostly on New Jersey. Their most realistic hope is to finish the Florida season with enough money to make the trip up North, and to finish the Northern season with enough money to make the trip back South. To find the possessors of this dreary hope, you must leave Route 441 on any of the side roads, follow to still smaller ones, get onto a rutted narrow pair of tire paths until you find the dead end—the huddling of tiny shacks like tribal hovels at an African jungle clearing.

This year desperation ran through the camps. One Thursday it began to rain in flooding sheets and two days later the last of the bean crop was ruined. It was a severe financial loss for the farmers. It meant starvation for the pickers: the last three weeks of the bean crop meant not only food to live on but the money to get to New Jersey for the summer.

Mildred Mason—not her real name—is a skinny girl, a second-generation migrant worker who knows what her life is headed for and wants to change it. She is eighteen years old; when only fifteen years old she had an illegitimate child who died in infancy from dysentery. This is not unusual. Mildred is now legally married—the certificate is tacked to their hovel wall—and appears to have a clear view of her life. This is unusual. She and her husband, Joe, are trying to leave the migrant life.

They live with their two children in a one-room shack whose roof—in the immemorial porosity of the rural slums —leaks. When it rains they all get out of bed and fold the bedsteads into a narrow dry corner. There are no windows, only hinged boards. Fleas and flies are so thick nobody troubles to brush them off. The children, two years and five months old, wake up at 6 a.m. crying from hunger. Joseph pulls on his trousers and starts the family heating system and cookstove—an open fire in front of the shack. Mildred draws water from the nearby pump that serves the twelve shacks in the camp. From the rusted refrigerator outside their shack she takes fatback and powdered milk and coffee—after unlocking the padlock. There is no electricity, of course, but the old box keeps rats away from the food. They may also eat whatever they can pick free from surrounding crops. Nearby some workers are eating diced raw okra for breakfast, dining from a tin plate set on top of an overturned bean basket.

The Masons and their fellows of the field are thin, the only large group of poor in America who are. This is partly because of their walking and stooping work in the heat. But it is mostly because they fail to reach the next-to-last stage of bad nutrition where most of the American poor reside, the level where cheap fatty fillers are used to keep away hunger pangs. The migrant workers aren't that well off. Besides, they eat a great deal of the free crops they pick—vegetables and fruits.

By 8 or 9 a.m. the dew is off the field and they walk or ride a truck to the crop. If they are well off, by migrant standards, they leave the two children with an immobile migrant woman of their camp who charges $1 a day per child for baby-sitting. If they are badly off they take the children with them and Mrs. Mason divides her time and nervous system between the piecework of the fields and keeping an eye on two unattended children who crawl in the dirt.

Mr. Mason can make $36 to $42 a week. With green beans they get 50 to 70 cents a basket, depending on the fullness of the crop. The labor contractor, standing at the rear of the truck, pays out the cash from a money changer at his waist, basket for basket, as the workers deliver them. Mrs. Mason may make $20 or $30, half of which may go to baby-sitters.

She spends about $18 a week for food, and on a combined weekly income of $50 this would leave something for civilization, especially since they live rent-free. But no migrant worker makes this every week. The life of the field worker rests upon the whimsy of the weather—the date a crop ripens, the days of rain when there is no picking or weeding, storms, gaps between crops—and the inexorable invasion of the fields by machines.

In 1959 the average days worked for all migrant workers was 143. These 143 days represent no weekly pay based on working five days out of seven. A migrant gets paid only when he works, only for the full basket he delivers to the truck. When he works he works twelve hours a day, seven days a week, for he knows there will be long stretches—a majority of his life—when there will be no pay at all.

The number of working days gets shorter with each passing year. Automatic machinery is learning to plant, weed, and pick. At the very least it has established a competitor to the human picker, so that when living hands try to increase their rate of pay to keep up with the steady rise in the cost of living they can be foiled by the cut-off point at which it becomes profitable for the farmer to switch to machinery. At worst the machine replaces the worker completely. A worker used to get $3.05 for picking 100 pounds of seed cotton. But since 1952 when the machines began to come in—at a cost of $20,000 a machine for the farmer—it became cheaper to use the machine, if human rates reached $2.50 per 100 pounds. Since 1952 the human rate has never gone over $2.80 and is usually below that. In general, the machine picks the easy crops where workers made most of their money in the past. Afterward the human beings pick what the machine missed, or work in fields so unevenly grown that machines don't do well and where human beings, too, have troubles. In 1950 about 92 per cent of American cotton was picked by human hands; in 1954, 33 per cent. Cotton used to be a $6-a-day crop six months a year. Now, thanks to scientific breeding of seed, chemical weed killers, technical control of growing season, and machine-working of the fields, human beings are needed only sixty days.

All through America's fields, science and technology grow like healthy giants. In Maine in 1954, 8000 workers harvested snap beans, in 1960 only 1400. In Massachusetts machines picked only 10 per cent of the cranberries in 1954, displacing only 300 people; by 1960 machines picked 63 per cent, displacing 2600 workers. In Michigan in 1956, 14,000 people picked snap beans; in 1960, 2800 picked a larger crop. In Iowa the sugar beet harvest is now 100 per cent mechanized. In ten years human beings employed to pick Iowa's corn dropped from 30,000 to 13,000 mainly because a new seed was developed that eliminated the process of detasseling the ear. From 1950 to 1960 these numbers of human beings were replaced by machines in the state of Louisiana: 50,000 cotton workers, 25,000 sugar cane harvesters, 15,000 rice harvesters, 13,000 rice planters, and 7000 sweet potato harvesters, for a total of 110,000.

But the number of human beings whose life and death depends on working the crops is not declining. In 1959 there were 30 per cent more migrant farm workers than in 1952. Like the Masons, most came from sharecropping where there was no work whatever. They come from the small farms, from the villages where no cash at all can be earned. In desperation some shift from farm to migrant camp and then try the city, only to find none of the three will support life. One group of ex-farmers-turned-migrant-workers settled in the Philadelphia slums and, facing starvation there, began migrating to nearby Pennsylvania and New Jersey farms for harvesting, combining the worst of two worlds—slum and migrant camp. Others have been luckier and have disappeared from the migrant maps. In Wapato, Washington some 1500 migrant Mexican-Americans now constitute half the population of that town, having dropped out of the migrant stream to take up ranching, barbering, store clerking, and odd jobs in a community that happened to be able to absorb them.

For most migrant workers the idle days increase but still the gap widens between them and the ever-rising platform of American industrial skills. In the days of doing nothing they sit at the edges of the camps or drink cheap wine or lounge in the sagging old buses, dressed in rags, leaving fleas untouched on nose and eyelash, trying to stay out of the sun, and waiting for word that somewhere another crop is ready.

"*In Louisiana,*" said Honey, a tall, sad Negro of thirty-eight, "*there hain't nothing to work at and it gets tiresome for a boy to jess look at the same ole place and same ole folks and same ole nothing to do. So I heard there was jobs in Florida an' I went. Been here ever since.*"

A slender Georgian hunched his shoulders and looked out the broken bus window at the aluminum-sided shacks, the waving ten-foot grass, the children all but naked playing in the dust with cardboard boxes.

"*Hell, I just wanted to see the world.*"

Had he seen the world?

"*Yeh, I seen it.*"

Did he want to keep seeing it this way?

"*What else is there for me to do?*"

The Masons, too, are caught in the silent tide of scientific change, conscious only that somehow there seem to be more days between crops, less money at the end of each year.

Last year at the end of May, with the beans finished in Florida, the Masons headed North. Mr. Mason drove another man's old station wagon to pay for his fare. It cost

$5 for Mrs. Mason, then pregnant, and her small child. They left Florida one May afternoon, $25 in their pockets—their net for the winter's work—and went up the road toward New Jersey. Inside the station wagon went all their possessions they could carry—a television set (an "inherited" one, for the Jersey camps with electricity), three trunks, some pots and pans, and a cardboard box of clothes. Padlocked in their old shack were two pieces of torn stuffed furniture, two cots, the non-operating refrigerator, a wooden table, and one wooden chair. (When they returned in the fall the shack, not unexpectedly, had been broken into and all the furnishings stolen.)

After driving day and night for two days, eating hamburgers and hot dogs along the way, they arrived in Cedarville, New Jersey. They had $14 left. They discovered that the New Jersey strawberry crop was unexpectedly ten days late. They lived in the shacks by the strawberry fields and eked out their $14.

When the strawberries finally ripened, the Masons were almost penniless and, once again, they paid the penalty of indebtedness. Pay was $6 for every 100 quarts picked, but it was in the form of a ticket issued for every ten boxes delivered to the truck. The tickets were worth 60 cents—if saved up and turned in all at one time at the end of the week. Mr. Mason picked 800 tickets' worth the first week. Mrs. Mason, in early pregnancy and sick, couldn't work at first. Since they had no money, they could not save their tickets for their full cash equivalent. Instead they had to use the tickets to buy food at the end of each day. The only place the tickets could be used as tender was at a farm commissary, and there the tickets were worth 55 cents, not 60. Thus, their need to use the tickets at once rather than save them until week's end, cost them more than 8 cents on every dollar earned.

Being behind from the start, they stayed that way most of the season. At week's end they were lucky to have fifty tickets unspent. After strawberries, their favorite Jersey crop, came the hated onion which needs slashing with a knife. Mrs. Mason was often sick in the fields. In late August they headed back South, arriving at the broken door of the Florida shack with $3 to show for the summer's work.

The Masons have just finished another winter. Because of the two days of heavy rain and the lost bean crop, they have nothing. They live on an occasional handout from the Migrant Missionary Fellowship, a non-denominational mission run by William Bell and his wife. Nearby towns have been scoured for jobs; there are, for all practical purposes, none.

Mildred Mason is slender, solemn and possessed of uncommon poise. But now she spoke in a rush.

"I don't want my husband picking crops any more and I don't want my children to. My mother did and she still does. Now I'm doing it. But I don't want my kids to. I'm tired of worrying about crops being ready, worrying if it's going to rain, worrying if there'll be a storm. I want food for my kids, a house that doesn't have rats or bugs, that has windows in it, a house where the wind won't come through the wall and the rain comes in like there was no roof at all. I want my kids to have an education. It's awfully hard to get a job without an education. We can both tell you that. What I really want is for my husband to have a

steady job where he won't have to worry are there too many pickers to make a good day's pay, is it going to rain, is the crop going to be late. It's hard work and we're good pickers. But I never had in my whole life more than $40 cash at one time. Right now I don't have a single penny."

Her eyes filled and she looked fierce as her six-month-old child crawled to her feet and stuck a fist into his mouth.

"I don't have a single penny and no food. But I don't care. I don't want to go up that road any more."

CHAPTER TEN

"I want my boys to come home."

Jose Chico is a powerful, barrel-shaped American Indian born, as closely as he can calculate, around 1902. He isn't sure of the precise date because Indian births in those days were not recorded and those who were baptised were admitted into Christian communion in collective anonymity as one of a group of, say, "ten Indians." His estimate of age is based on a reference by elders in his village to 1906, the year of some unremembered phenomenon from which lesser events of the era were measured. They used to tell him that in 1906 "you were that high" and hold their arms almost straight down with palms outstretched. The indicated height leads him to think he must have been four years old at the time.

I first met Jose Chico beside a mission church in the middle of the desert as he watched, passively, two baseball teams of Papagos Indians, one in uniforms marked "The Rangers" and the other, "The Papagos Trading Post." Jose Chico was dressed like any other Arizona dirt farmer: blue jeans, green cotton shirt, a sombrero. Our introduction was slow, tentative, and reserved, a process in which I took no part for half an hour. During that time the older man listened casually, patiently, then with more intensity to Eugene Johnson, the young elected chairman of the tribal council who had taken a day or so himself to gain confidence in my mission. I was, after all, pressing against a shield most Indians use against intrusion into their personal lives by outsiders. The Papagos are part of a larger family of Indians, the Pima, a name that may have come from their persistent response to questions of the Spanish conquistadores, "Pi-nyi-maach," or "I don't know," a trilogy of words still heard by outsiders in the 1960's. After a long time, the two men approached and introductions were made, the old man speaking in Papagos and Mr. Johnson translating to English. We talked, he forgetting the ball game and I trying to ignore spectacular fielding, until the old man while describing his childhood said he had attended eighth grade in the Bureau of Indian Affairs school in New Mexico. *"But that means you speak English,"* I said.

Jose Chico looked at me calmly and with only a slight blink said, *"Yes."* Thereafter we spoke English.

Jose Chico is important to the story of the poor because he represents the 500,000 Indians of the United States, almost all of them impoverished. The comic strips concentrate on the few oil-and-uranium Indians; the Indian of American humor is the millionaire Kickapoo from Oklahoma who buys Kansas City hotels for the night. In literature it is, "Lo, the poor Indian!" of Alexander Pope whose adjective "poor" is ironic because the Indian is rich in spirit. But the dominant economic fact about the American Indian is that he is extremely poor and this, inexorably, is corroding his spirit.

But Jose Chico has a larger significance than that. In the cold priorities of statistics, the Indians are less than 2 per cent of the American poor. Yet they demonstrate as dramatically as any single group the root cause of modern poverty in the United States: cultural obsolescence, the swift tide of change that has left previously proud, competent, and productive peoples useless and unused, not because they have changed but because the world has, not just because they adjust slowly, but because every year the rate of change accelerates and obsolescence penetrates more deeply into every nook and cranny of society.

Even in the land of the Papagos, the 4000 square miles of Arizona along the Mexican border, one of the most inaccessible inhabited domains in the country, there is no hiding from the irresistible tide. The stronger the old culture, the more tragic its envelopment. What used to be good is now bad, what was once noble is now humiliating, what had been celebrated for generations as the height of skill is now incompetence. In greater or lesser degree this is the story of the great body of the American poor: the small farmer, the Southern Negro, the Southern rural white, the small-town family thrust into the city. Jose Chico, feeling the ground crumble beneath him but clinging to what he knows and loves, is a symbol of what is happening to most of the 36,000,000 poor.

For the first thirty years of his life he lived as did the rest of the tribe the same way the Papagos did in 1500 A.D. In summer, families lived in adobe houses on the upland plains, a few cattle grazing on desert vegetation, the women coaxing from the begrudging soil enough corn and beans and squash to last from spring to autumn. Then they moved to the mountains for the winter where the men hunted deer, rabbit, and mountain goat, and the women picked native foods: acorns, pinion nuts, juniper berries, and, lower down, mesquite beans and the tender buds of the cholla cactus. They lived in clusters of tiny villages, each ruled by a patriarch. Their medical or spiritual ills (they made no distinction) were treated largely by medicine men and singing healers, as they probably were through most of the 5000 years anthropologists believe the Papagos and their forebears have been there. Their skills were those of the hunter, of the subsistence farmer, the cowherd, of a people so entwined with the subtle, brutal, and beautiful desert that they could live off the land unaided. They were a peaceful and sedentary tribe, unlike their enemy, the Apaches, but in their own way they were magnificent examples of the ingenuity of man, of sensitivity to nature, and the endurance of a human society in a cruel environment. Their code of conduct was attuned to the realities of this world: devotion to family and blood relation and to the tribe, not to the individual. Acts affecting all should be approved by all, though the elders decided what was the sense of the people. Extreme caution with strangers was basic, its roots in the religion in which hostile spirits could exploit personal knowledge, not to mention the atavistic memories of the treachery of the Spaniards, the Apaches, and the white man. The self-proclaimed big shot is reviled, personal modesty exalted. Gaining for oneself at the expense of another is shameful. The Papagos survived because these tenets became the nucleus of the Papagos personality.

To the casual eye it is not so different today. The desert, the adobe houses, the slow-moving women in the fields, the dry cattle look the same. But the dynamic new ingredients are there. White standards no longer tolerate a view of the Indian as a second-class citizen ordained to misery. By 1933 the Federal government decided it had more than a policeman's role to play and in Sells, seat of the reservation, the Bureau of Indian Affairs bustles with plans and surveys, always presented diplomatically as advice to a self-ruling people. Cultures collide with the help of radio, television, the automobile, the turmoil of World War II, and the ferment of education. In an ethical nation, both sides responded by wanting to do the "right thing," but what was right? For the Indian there was a vision of a new life—healthy children, longer life, modern education, success by outer world standards. This required cash, but their land was without resources for cash. It required something even deeper: a new culture. Men who reached adulthood by one code of conduct faced failure if they followed it thereafter. The centuries-old measures of honor—obedience to elders, rejection of personal ambition, disdain for individual possessions—became marks of failure in a highly competitive white collar world. The instinctive love for the land remained but it struggled with the desire to succeed by new standards. The superb hunter, the meticulous cowherd, the desert farmer representing generations of acquired knowledge of a unique land was now faced with an automated, asphalted, missile-protected, applicationed-in-triplicate, graduate-degree society. It was as though a man went to sleep in a mountain hut of Spain in the time of Columbus and woke up in a Chicago slum the day an astronaut orbited the earth.

For the Indian it has become the world of the sacred eagle feather and Coca-Cola all mixed up in one. It is still commonly expected in the villages that a baby born in summer will get infant diarrhea and probably die, but that this may be arrested by a medicine man. The dehydrated baby's skull sinks in and the traditional treatment is for the medicine man to sing an incantation, to stroke the skull with a sacred feather, then to press his thumb upward on the child's palate to attempt a maximum ballooning of the soft cranium and fill whatever depression is left on top of the head with a sacred white glue. This is still done. But if the treatment fails it is declared "a white man's sickness" and the child, if he is seen soon enough by the public health nurse on the weekly visit, is sent to the 50-bed airconditioned U.S. Public Health Service hospital in Sells, where he is treated by a bright young graduate of the Harvard Medical School.

The Papagos live in natural splendor of the Arizona desert, 4000 square miles of purple mesa and bright color. One of their sources of income is rent on Kitt Peak, the 6800-foot mountain they lease to the Associated Universities for Research in Astronomy where there is now the world's largest sunscope, visible white and gleaming for miles around, an elevated island of Ph.D.s in the sky. The gate to the mountain road is marked closed at 4 p.m. but when we drove up at 5 p.m. the chairman of the tribal council could say in his only immodest announcement in days, *"They had better let us in or else I'll kick them off my mountain."* From the top of the peak, the rolling desert and distant mountains were so beautiful that even the tribal chairman who had seen them all his life was transfixed and only after many minutes said sadly and proudly, "As far as your eye can see belongs to our people." But, the per capita income of the Papagos people is $440 a year, one-fifth that of the average American, and they suffer from disease and dietary deficiency.

Jose Chico is one of the 11,000 Papagos in this world who own these awesome 3,000,000 acres. He is one of the 7000 who live permanently on the reservation, in his well-made adobe house, with his wife and five children. He has five horses and two cows and no regular cash-paying job. He herds some cattle for others, helps neighbors build and repair their homes, and somehow nurses out of the arid soil a garden of squash, beans, watermelon and wheat (which he grinds himself). Once a month he gets a welfare allotment of surplus foods but this never lasts the whole month, so he needs to pay cash for some food. The cash comes mostly from picking cotton at the edge of the reservation, but this work is reduced every year by introduction of automatic machinery in the fields. He thinks he earns about $500 cash a year (and perhaps as much in equivalent mutual help from those whose houses he repairs or payment in tools and food). He buys coffee, sugar, salt, and now and then some hamburger or other cheap meat. He has the usual small-store expense of the isolated poor: the mimeographed "Papago Indian News" had grocery advertisements, one for a Tucson supermarket, beyond the range of Papagos without cars, selling one pound of Folger's coffee for 59 cents; another for the local "Indian Oasis Trading Post & Service Station," selling one pound of Folger's coffee for 69 cents.

"*My father had a better life, more food, was more sure of everything,*" he said. For one thing, there seemed to be more rain then, providing more grass for cattle and more gardening; the local Bureau of Indian Affairs agrees that this generation seems to be suffering a dry cycle. The grazing for cattle is close to the Chico family economy for cattle represent a Papagos' savings account. Here, too, the economy of the poor bears down hard. The Papagos ranges will carry about 11,000 cattle properly. But because they are economically pressed, the Papagos have tried to improve their lot in the only means at hand—their own cattle and their own land. Today they have 18,000 in their herds. These have overgrazed, cutting down the sparse vegetation holding the soil. At the same time, they leased grazing land to white cattlemen who also overgrazed. Towns and cities just outside the reservation deepened their wells and increased their pumping so that water became harder than ever to get to the surface inside the reservation. In 1916 there were 9000 acres of the reservation irrigated and productive; now there are less than 3000. In this generation nine inches of topsoil have been lost from 250,000 acres. As so often happens, the impulse to close the gap between what one has and what one needs only diminishes what one has.

For Jose Chico, as for all the poor, shoes are an economic lightning bolt on the family budget. He is cautious and thrifty, saving what he can for emergencies. He had saved $30 for food in May when he received a letter from the mission school in New Mexico where his two older sons are in high school. There is no public high school on the reservation. The Catholic Church pays the boys' tuition and upkeep but their father pays for their transportation and clothes. It costs him $51 for them to go to school by bus in September, and $51 for them to return in

June. The forthcoming June $51 already was going to be a family crisis. But the letter in April was unexpected: both boys needed new shoes. So most of the food money for May was mailed out and the family will have to live on their surplus food allotment, which is about half their usual diet. *"They need shoes, to stay in school. What can you do?"*

How will they come home for the summer?

"I want my boys to come home. I never see them during the year. This is the only time I see them."

How will he find the $51 bus fare?

Jose Chico looked solemn and said, *"I will have to sell a cow."* This was a grave statement. For a Papagos with two cows to sell one is like a Bostonian spending half his capital at one crack.

Life could be harder. There is a well near Jose Chico's home. Some Papagos are not so lucky. Albert Jose lives in the village of Big Fields, has four children of school age, and works when he can in the cotton fields. But he has to spend one day a week providing his family with water. He hitches two of his three horses to the old wagon and drives them to the well, five miles from his home, fills three large barrels in the wagon and returns home. This is his water for one week. Albert Jose's village has no electricity and no water.

The Public Health Service is ready to pipe water near Big Fields but the village elders have not yet approved. They are still pondering the motives and consequences of the white man's act. To some this appears to be panicked obstructionism: for families barely able to get enough food for their children, a whole day's work a week to obtain

water is a lavish waste of time. But in the conflict between the old ways and the new the white man has neither let the Indian alone nor worked with him with any
constancy. The history of the white man's ways is vivid
in the old men's memories. Three generations ago, for example, the railroad went through Arizona and employed
the Indians at high cash wages. There was plenty of work
and Indians were urged to follow the laying of the iron
rails in order to give themselves and their sons and their
grandsons money and food. So houses were abandoned,
gardens let go, cattle slaughtered and families moved to
where the white man's work beckoned. And then the railroad was completed and there was no work, no cash, and
the Indians had no homes or gardens or cattle. When the
village kept postponing the faucet that Public Health
Service men wanted to install, a thoughtful government
man who had quietly gained the confidence of the village
leader asked why it was not welcomed.

"He told me about the railroad," the government man
recalled. "And then he told me about another water project
the government had around the first World War. The government in Washington wanted to build some dams in the
hills to make a reservoir to provide water for the tribe and
for some irrigation. The construction would mean cash
wages, too. Well, the old men said they had doubts about
that. For centuries the Papagos have been experts at divert-
ing flash floods and they preferred the old ways. But the
government engineers won out. They started building the
dam.

"Then one autumn they had a downpour and one of
the unfinished dams collected a lot of water behind it and

*let go. It washed away a whole village. Never before in the
memory of the tribe had that happened. So now I understand better why they're pretty slow to accept the white
man's ways. This is their whole world and their whole history. A little flood out in Southern Arizona is nothing much
to you or me but to them it was their whole world under-
water, sort of like the flood in the Bible and they'll remember it that long, too."*

Nevertheless, slowly and inexorably change comes.
When the new hospital was opened in 1961 among the
first official visitors was a delegation of village medicine
men—they wore slacks and sports shirts, no wild feather
headdresses—who dutifully looked at the operating room,
the emergency clinic, the X-ray chambers, the oxygen tents,
and then went back to the villages to practice their old
rituals with animal hides and eagle feathers. But when
these fail they are quicker, or so it seems to the hospital
doctors, to declare the patient afflicted not with an Indian ailment but a "white man's sickness" and let the visiting nurse look at him.

It is easy to sentimentalize the old ways as automatic
wisdom. But such ways are not without wisdom. It is, for
example, obvious that Papagos children need a high school.
The Bureau of Indian Affairs has for years been prepared
to build one. At present parents who are able send their
children to boarding school, either Catholic ones in New
Mexico or those run by the government for Indians far
from the Papago reservation. This limits the number who
can attend and, by placing an exorbitant cost on education,
cripples the next generation's efforts to survive economically. Yet for over a year the elders have failed to come to a

decision on the new school. The talks go on endlessly. In the Indian fashion, even the children are asked their opinion. If some say no, there is no decision, for all must acquiesce. For the men who worry about teen-agers on the reservation who can find no work, or who wander uneducated into Phoenix and Tucson to become drunks or pool sharks or petty thieves, this is maddening.

But what do the old men say when they are asked about their delay? They ask what will happen to the children from villages like Ali Chuk that is ninety miles from Sells or Gu Vo that is seventy-five miles away? Will they have to be away from their homes and families while they are becoming young men? Will the new school ridicule the old ways? Will it prepare them for white man's work which they will not be able to find and thus leave them dissatisfied with both the old and the new? If it is true that the old ways must go, then is it wise to send them to a strictly Indian school or would it be better to send them to a white man's school where they will learn not only white men's ways but also come to know white men's children and the white men's children come to know the Indian?

While the tides of change pull at the fringes of Indian living, at the center—the home—the immemorial rhythm continues. Early in the morning the mother gets up and starts a wood fire in the outdoor stove under a roofed portal. In good times breakfast may be fried potatoes, Mexican beans, tortillas, and coffee. Lunch may be beans, tortillas, and coffee. If deer has been caught there will be some, usually dried. Or rabbit, though it is believed to be unhealthy to eat rabbit several days in succession. (But most Papagos men still hunt regularly for deer and rabbit as part of their regular diet.) In the evening there are leftovers and perhaps pinole—a roasted wheat germ mixed with water or milk. There may be cholla cactus buds.

The family is strong, loyalty to kin unquestioned, and within these groups there is much sharing of food and clothing. It is considered shameful for a man to eat while somewhere a blood relative goes hungry. The oldest man is head of the household except where he is plainly lacking in strength or leadership—then authority devolves in some mysterious way to the most able male.

This is not a bad way of life. It has many of the elements that thoughtful leaders of white society perpetually call for—a regard for one's fellow man, devotion to family, an order of life that includes justice and compassion, a closeness to nature, and an exaltation of beauty.

Yet the painful problems of the Papagos can be solved, so far as anyone can see, only by the destruction of the society that produced these values.

There are about 1200 families among the Papagos of which about 400 have enough white man's education and training to deal with the outside world, that is, work steadily, or else get a steady living within the reservation. This top third of the Papagos have a standard of living about half that of the average non-Indian in Arizona.

The other 800 families live even further below the subsistence level for modern United States. They hang on by cultivating tiny gardens, raising small herds of cattle, cutting wood, occasionally picking cotton. Many—about 40 per cent of the Papagos—speak no English. They are destitute enough to follow any hint of work; whole families move temporarily to the cotton fields and odd jobs near the reservation, these migrations further burdening their children with interrupted education and lack of health services. Their plight is getting worse, not better. A government worker on the reservation says:

"Half the families here used to get cash working in the cotton fields. But mechanization has cut that down to less than 100 families and each of these make less than $1000 a year on it."

The spiritual richness of much Indian life is real, but it does not wipe away the tragic cost of economic poverty. In 1948, 258 of every 1000 newborn Papagos died in infancy, six times the average rate for other Americans. If a baby survived he could expect to die at age seventeen; other Americans lived to be sixty-nine.

This is a grim cost of poverty, but it is largely avoidable tragedy. Modern health services and surplus government food were introduced. By 1955 the infant death rate had dropped from 258 to ninety-seven, and by now it is below eighty-five, an enormous saving of life and prevention of family tragedy, though the rate is still three times the general American average. By 1956 the average age at death for a Papagos was thirty-three years, by 1959 it was forty-one, and by now, as one doctor said, it might be as high as fifty years of age. Obviously, Jose Chico was a statistical freak, a rare man who had cheated the odds.

There are still obvious improvements to be made. Lack of sanitation and poor diets still create massive health problems. Indians are generally fat for the same reason most of the American poor are fat: they stave off hunger with the cheapest starchy fillers. Though the Federal government provides free surplus foods (beans, flour, peanut butter, lard, whole wheat, rice), these are distributed by the state of Arizona whose trucks make deliveries to only 11 of the forty-four villages; some people have to travel twenty miles to get their food. Half the eligible Papagos can't get to the food or don't know how to apply for it. The cost of this is not small.

Twenty-five per cent of all Papagos have diabetes which causes cataracts, kidney disease, premature hardening of the arteries. It is the highest rate in the United States, caused by a large carbohydrate intake plus years of too close breeding. Another 15 per cent have gall bladder disease, 250 per cent higher than the U.S. rate, caused, again, by obesity from starchy diets, and many pregnancies. Tuberculosis and chronic lung disease are three times the ordinary American rate. Dr. S. C. Binder, the young Harvard graduate who runs the hospital, said, "*When I came from Boston I had to get used to something. Lung X-rays we had come to expect from sick old men in the cities are common among young kids here. The scars most people collect in a lifetime of pneumonia, deep colds and lung infections, these kids have before they're twelve years old.*"

The choice between the old social order with its revered values and the modern world of a money economy is not an easy one. If one chooses the old he also takes dead babies, ailing adults and early death. If he chooses the new way—modern education and health—he will almost certainly destroy an ancient and still strong culture.

"*There are 1200 families here who have breadwinners in them who want work and can't find it. Half of these are the heads of their households,*" an employment officer of the Bureau of Indian Affairs told me.

As he talked I could see on a nearby hillside two old women and a younger one moving silently among the cacti and mesquite looking for edible buds. I wondered, with my new knowledge, how old the "old" women really were, whether they had in fact lived many years or were, instead, merely closer to death.

"*You know the answer,*" my informant behind the oak desk said, "*education and training. When their kids go to high school they'll learn to be radio repairmen, X-ray technicians, auto mechanics, welders, secretaries. But this will mean the end of the tribal structure and of life as we know it on the reservation today. A good welder or an engineer or a stenographer isn't going to find work on the reservation. That kind of job is out in the cities, far from here. That means the end of the family structure, of everything the kids grew up with. It's hard to see where it will all lead to.*"

Dr. William H. Kelly, director of the Bureau of Ethnic Research of the University of Arizona, says that about 5800 Papagos live or work off the reservation already, but that most of them have no training in skilled jobs and live in poverty. Off the reservation, alcoholism is high, families fall apart, and prostitution and promiscuity are common.

"*For the next two generations,*" he said, "*it can be taken for granted that any Indian without a high school diploma and good vocational technical training is doomed to be a common laborer. Remember that the Papagos population is now doubling every fifteen years, thanks to the new hospital and government foods, and also that as the years go by there will be a decreasing number of jobs in common laboring. Very few Indians are being reached by any program that will prepare them for this. Life is going*

*to be very hard for many years to come. Life for the Indian
500 years ago, hell, 50 years ago, was predictable—hard but
predictable. He knew what it was all about and he faced it.
Generations had the same problems and worked out the
best answers. Suddenly life is no longer predictable."*

It is little wonder that the elders hesitate about the
new high school. It is a bitter choice: love and duty within
the family at the cost of near-starvation, or modern wage-
earning and the end of five centuries of a noble heritage.

Jose Chico, already a rarity among the Papagos because he had lived to be sixty-two, stood by the corner of
his neat corral constructed of great cactus ribs and the
thorny branches of the ocotillo bush. Inside the compound
was a well-made adobe house, the packed earth around it
swept clean, the outdoor cooking ramada hung with pans,
the stage of a lifetime, of a tribal history of uncounted generations, a monument to his successful struggle against
the desert. You could see the cataracts in his eyes as he
looked out somberly as the evening sun glided against the
cactus on the valley floor. We talked of his two sons in
New Mexico and as we talked he became more somber.

What did his children plan to do for a living after they
finished high school in New Mexico?

Jose Chico stared as long as it is courteous to look at
another man without speaking. Then he looked back at
the shadows stretching out over the desert.

*"I don' know. Come back home with me. I think.
Maybe. I hope."*

CHAPTER ELEVEN

"Why, there's not enough money here for prostitution . . ."

"I'm going to be a lawyer," said Harry, aged six. "Lawyers make good money. I'm going to keep my money."

"I'm going to be a doctor," said his seven-year-old brother firmly. "And I'm going to take care of my family."

Their eight-year-old sister announced serenely:

"I'm going to be a nurse in a big hospital and wear a real uniform and help people."

The sweet optimism of youth could have been heard in millions of homes, but this home was rather special.

It was midafternoon but the tenement was dark. Grey plastic sheeting was tacked to the insides of the living room windows except for one window where a stick was propped against the collapsed Venetian blind to keep it against the cracked glass. Plaster was off an expanse of ceiling and walls, and strands of hair on the laths trembled with the passing wind from outside. A double doorway gave onto the kitchen which was almost invisible. Its windows, too, were sealed with grey plastic, presumably to preserve heat. But the darkness was thickened by a criss-cross of clotheslines that filled the room with the hangings of what looked like shapeless cloth. In one corner of the kitchen was a small refrigerator, in another a table with three legs and one chair. There was a stained stove bearing a basin full of children's clothes soaked in cold soapy water. Next to the clothes basin was a pan of cold red beans and beside that an iron frying pan containing a single short rib congealed with fat. Through one kitchen door was a bathroom dominated by a toilet covered by boards; it had frozen and burst during the winter. Through another door was "the kids' room," a murky chamber with one window insulated by a roller shade tacked at the top and held down at the bottom sill with a stone. In this room slept seven children, in two beds. Neither bed had a mattress. The children slept on the springs.

"*Look at this book I got from school,*" Harry said, calling from the living room. "*Want to hear me read?*"

Harry read about Dick and Jane and their dog, Spot. Dick and Jane were cleancut, well-dressed, blonde and red-headed Anglo-Saxon children who lived behind a white picket fence in a red-roofed cottage with geraniums in the window. Their mother was a smiling blonde with clear, square teeth. The father wore a snap brim hat, a conservative suit, and carried a briefcase. And they all lived happily in a schoolbook called *Friends and Neighbors*.

Little Harry might as well have read science fiction about Mars. He had never seen a cottage like that, never knew such parents of his own or anyone else, and so far as one could tell had never seen a geranium or a father in a business suit. His own family, for example, had never in his memory eaten a meal together. There weren't enough chairs, dishes, or forks. But Harry was still eager to please. He had not yet learned that other people expected him to be like Dick and his sister to be like Jane, and expected them to have parents like Dick's and Jane's, to live in a house like Dick's and Jane's, and that as a Negro slum kid all of this was as remote to him as the canals of Mars. And unless he was uncommonly lucky, this book and the school it came from would soon seem as remote.

Harry's mother, Mrs. Martin—to use a fictitious name that will not further burden young Harry—is a weary, round-faced, bewildered woman of indeterminate age in appearance but only twenty-seven. Conversation swirled without touching her most of the time, her brow perpetually creased, a half-smile in constant apology. She looked toward the tangle of clothes hanging from the kitchen ropes.

"The school, they said the kids' clothes had gotta be cleaner and better. Ah kep' theys clothes jess as clean as ah could but now ah washes 'em every night. Kids they get undressed about five-thirty an' then ah washes. Ah gets up at six in the mornin' and sometimes ah irons what ah washed an' hung the night before."

The Martins are on welfare, aid to dependent children of the unemployed. Their father is seen spasmodically. He is usually drunk. Mrs. Martin is overwhelmed by the household and trying to deal with the outside world, so she is one of the rare cases in which the welfare workers pay most of the bills directly, the $75 a month for rent, the gas and electric bills as they come due, and the $9.45 a month for "household incidentals." She gets $151.90 a month for food for eight.

The father has been drunk most of the time since the winter of 1962. That was when the meat packing company where he had worked for seven years moved to another city

with an automated plant. And it was the winter the youngest child, a boy of five months who slept in a supermarket
basket for a crib, died of pneumonia.

"We come from McCrory, Arkansas," Mrs. Martin
said. *"We'd been born there an' we was 'croppin'. It was
pretty bad. We had two kids and they wasn't nothing to
eat and the place we lived in, well it rained right in all the
time an' we jess had things worse an' worse gettin' seed and
fertilizer. 'Bout a year before, mah husban's brother, he
come up here to Chicago to work in this meat packin' plant
and he wrote back to McCrory and said we should come
up. So we did an' at first we stayed with his brother. They
had a four-room place here on the West Side and he and
his wife and their seven kids they used three of the rooms
and my husband and me and the two kids we used the other
room. It was that way for about a month, yes I guess it was
a month until we got the first pay and we found ourselves
a house. The pay, it was $84 a week. We was doing right
well."*

She talked without change of expression, or lifting
of voice, as though it were a recitation of events that happened to someone else one hundred years ago. She looked
weary and apathetic, huddling in the perpetual twilight
of her tenement. She seemed always to be counting the
children silently and looking over her shoulder. When a
footstep is heard outside the children run to a living room
window looking over the entryway to the building, the outside stairway faded and fuzzy through the plastic sheeting
and the crusted window. *"Don' go out, don' go out,"* the
mother repeats, though no child makes a move to go
out. She keeps them in the flat, away from the bleak and

melancholy streets. But on the way to school the older children keep their eyes open for an unbroken soda bottle in the carpeting litter over sidewalk and street, for such a bottle may bring a 2-cent deposit and enough of these will buy a packaged cupcake or a soda at the basement variety store, an event announced with a thunderclap to the awed children at home. But Mrs. Martin says, "*Don' go out, don' go out,*" because in the alleys there are dangers worse than broken glass.

So when footsteps are heard on the front stoop the children run to the window, their eyes excited. It could be a stranger with something different and exotic; it might be Sister Mary William, the tall tough-talking young Irish nun with a candy cane and words with their mother; it may be their father and he could be all right or he could be drunk and there would be fighting and his demanding money and the children screaming. So the children's eyes are always bright at the window and Mrs. Martin says, "*Don' go out, don' go out.*" The footsteps go down the hallway, up the flight of stairs, and out of the Martins' worries.

It was time for them to get undressed. They eat their evening meal at 4 p.m. and are in bed by 8. In a tiny sector of the kitchen, an angle made by walls of clothes hanging on rope, the nun drew Mrs. Martin away from the children. The Irish girl's great peaked white hat ducked under the clothes and she straightened out afterward like a giant, her blue habit looming over the clothesline. "*I think,*" she said to Mrs. Martin slowly and discreetly, "*I'm going to arrange for you to get into a public housing project.*"

Mrs. Martin paused for a moment and then her face lifted. "*Public housing? Public housing? Oh, that would be*

*wonderful, jess wonderful. Public housing. You really think
so?"*

"Yes," the nun said, *"there's a place I think I can get
you in over on the South Side."*

Mrs. Martin's face froze. *"The South Side? The South
Side! Why, ah can't go to the South Side! Ah'd like to stay
on the West Side!"*

"Well," Sister Mary William said breezily, *"why don't
we wait and see how it turns out."*

The nun ducked under the clothesline and returned
to the children in the living room, leaving Mrs. Martin
alone with her thoughts in the gloom of her triangle of
clothes in the kitchen. She ducked under the clothesline
into another triangle near the kitchen stove. The suds had
disappeared in the cold basin of wash.

Did the children ever see television?

She looked at the visitor while she collected her
thoughts and said, *"Well, they see it sometimes at the
school and here and there. We ain't had one since I guess
maybe it was a year, no maybe two years, I don't rightly
remember, but he had jess got through paying for it, $300,
an' it was all paid for an' it broke down. We called the repair man an' he said he had to take it out to his shop. An'
the repair man, he came back with it the next Tuesday and
he had it out in his car an' give us the bill for $60. We din't
have no $60 then, right then that day, so he said to let him
know when we did. Well, we called him after that but he
done moved his shop an' never let us know his new address
so we never did see the TV after that."*

She would not talk of the baby that died except to

say that it was a terrible cold winter. *"The toilet it froze and busted from the cold. The radiator it din't hardly work. But the landlord he let us use another bathroom in the back an' don't charge us extra rent."*

Clothes for the children who go to school are a worry. When they need new shoes or clothing she has to wait until the welfare worker visits.

What about clothes for herself? When was the last time she bought a new dress? Until I asked that question it had been hard to remember that this was a twenty-seven-year-old woman, that a short time ago she came to the great city in eagerness. But now her eyes lost their emptiness and she smiled. Her voice carried as it had not before, so much so the children stopped talking in the living room and listened in amazement.

"It was six years ago. We was making good money at the meat plant an' he took me out to a dress shop. When he saw how much I really liked that dress he said, 'Honey, you get it.' It cost $30. Oh, that was a dress. I mean it really was a dress. It was pink and it was cut a lot lower than this one and it had sequins all over and they shined and shined and the pink was so pretty."

The girl from McCrory, Arkansas was for the first time identifiable with other young women, with a range of emotions, with liveliness in her voice. Then the face began to sag again and the crease returned to her forehead. She wiped her hands automatically on the side of her stained donated dress and one could see that her slip was held up with pieces of knotted twine.

" 'Bout three years ago we was staying in a place where

*they was leaks, worse than here. An' the dress, it was in a
closet where there was a awful leak an' it soaked the dress
through an' through. Ah din't know it an' the dress it got
mildewed an' I had to throw it out in the garbage."*

Outside, Sister Mary William looked down the endless line of row houses, at the trash barrels lolling on their
sides, the broken glass laid like a glistening carpet as far as
the eye could see. She crunched the broken glass under her
awkward black shoes and said:

*"You figure out what's going to happen to Harry
Martin when he finds out he's never going to be a lawyer.
And his brother's never going to be a doctor. And his sister's
never going to be a nurse. The worst most of us have to re-
sign ourselves to is that there's no Santa Claus. Wait until
this hits those kids."*

The sidewalk and street, strewn with paper and garbage and glittering with countless shards of broken glass,
stretched on and on, hemmed in by ragged row houses.
The smashed bottle has a morbid satisfaction for the
residents. Defiance. Retaliation. Seven years ago this neighborhood was almost entirely white, mostly Irish and
Italian, the houses unpretentious but fussily neat; what
are now black squares of packed earth covered with glass
were then ranks of green plots of grass, some with flowers
at the edge. The population supported huge churches,
cathedral-like in their domination of the Catholic neighborhood. Now they are gone, fled to suburban life or fashionable apartments, panicked at first by the appearance
of a few Puerto Ricans, this fear combined with a desire
to achieve the new status of garden apartment or single
home. The neighborhood is now 95 per cent Negro, the

churches, Catholic and Protestant, empty. The houses are packed.

"*The story of the poor is the story of real estate,*" Sister Mary William said as she looked into shadowed doorways where invisible child-voices cried out, "*Hi, Sister.*" "*These kids don't know what a Catholic is,*" she said, laughing. "*They and their parents still don't know. They keep asking if I have a husband and what I wear under my habit and what I use the big white cap for and is the priest really my father. But the poor know we live here with them and that we worry about them and that we're dependable. See that place there? Five rooms—you should see the rooms and what they call 'furnishings'—for $115 a month. Over there, two rooms furnished, $20 a week. You can see the rats come in through the holes in the wall. If you try to get something done you have trouble finding out who owns the building. Slum property is a gold mine. They're all ready for the wreckers, no taxes to speak of, no upkeep, and the rent per room is sky high. But some of them are just owned by trusts or company titles that lead you nowhere. I know some of them are owned by big aristocratic families or by those fine companies downtown. They hire managers to run their houses and the manager is the only man anyone here sees. And they usually see him on rent day and never any other time. Some managers do the best they can and some of them are rats.*

"*Last year I began running into conditions that were even worse than usual and believe me that means they were pretty bad. Rent going up every couple of months, crazy extra charges, and if they complain that there's no heat or the stairs have collapsed or the rats are biting the children they get lots of threats about bringing suit for damaging the property or going to get the welfare cut off. And pretty soon I found out that thirteen of the worst places were run by the same manager. It was the same in all thirteen places. So I talked to the women of the thirteen flats. You have lots more luck dealing with the women. They're home and they're lots more ready to fight, maybe because they've got the kids directly on their hands or because the men are lots more defeated. Of course, sometimes there just isn't any man, or at least not one you can pin down. And I got the thirteen women to withhold their rent on the same day. It took quite a lot of talking to get them to do it because these people are at the mercy of the outside and they feel alone. But I told them when the manager came for the rent, tell him they weren't paying this week and tell him to come see me. Well, I knew the day he'd be around and he came in like an atom bomb. He read me the riot act and then he pointed his finger at me and he said, 'And just for your information, I'm going right now to get you brought into court.' Before he could get his arm down I said, 'Good! That's just what I've been waiting for. I've been praying for that. Just let me get in front of a judge with the story of your tenements.' Well, he fixed up the flats pretty fast.*

"Now, over there two blocks over is a public housing project. Don't let anyone tell you the poor don't want public housing. The other people can complain about it but for the poor it's the promised land. Sure, they have trouble at first. Most of them never took care of a home in their lives. But we went in and organized Building Councils in each building. Every floor has a representative to the Council, elected by ballot and, brother, if you want to see democracy

in action you ought to see the campaign for Building Council. They have a Law and Order Committee and it cuts ice
with the families that get out of hand or who don't keep
their kids on the straight and narrow. When the Housing
Authority is going to have a fumigation, the Council gets
everyone ready at the right time and, believe me, that's a
tough job if you try to do it any other way. There's a lot
of venereal disease around here and when the Public Health
clinic comes around for blood tests, the Council gets everyone out. They've got a credit union and they set up a PTA.
If some family starts running rent parties that get rowdy,
the Council lowers the boom. This is their home and they
work for it."

The tall nun works out of an office she calls Rendu
House in the middle of the neighborhood, but it is an out-
post of a large establishment called Marillac House, a settlement house that grew in one of the abandoned edifices
of this formerly Catholic neighborhood. At Marillac House
she works with a young Negro college student, Gordon
Austin, who runs teen-age activities and adult education
classes. The twenty-year-old, mild-talking Austin found
himself immersed in something more than blackboard
exercises in the alphabet.

"We use a pretty good system to teach basic reading
and writing," he said, "but it's not all that simple. You
wouldn't believe how many of the parents in a neighborhood like this just never learned to read and write, or if they
did it was something done once for a few years when they
were in a one-room schoolhouse down South and then they
never used it again, like some kids taking a couple of years
of French. So they come up here where everyone takes it

for granted they can fill out forms, understand contracts, get written references for work. And they don't want to admit they can't read and write. Why, even when they come to register for writing class they try to fake their way by saying they left their glasses home.

"What it means with their kids is pretty serious. The last ones they want to admit it to is their own kids because already they've got trouble maintaining status with the kids. The kids may go to school. The parents may be out of work and look like failures anyway. The kids are full of questions the parents can't answer. So the first thing the parents do is make sure there's no printed material in the house, no newspapers or magazines or even comic books, because the kids might ask the parents something about it. The kid first begins to suspect it, lots of times, when he brings home a mimeographed notice from school or a report card. The parent may get angry and say he's busy, or tell the kid to take care of it himself. But sooner or later it dawns on the kid that his own mother or his own father can't read. And maybe he doesn't even know where to sign the report card. In some cases he can't sign it. I've seen this happen and it's quite a shock to a kid. He loses a lot of respect for the parent and he begins to doubt that his parent has anything at all to say to him. You begin to see real contempt, sometimes.

"This means the parents are easy marks for the sharpies selling stuff on the installment plan. You know, on a lot of charge account forms and sales contracts, the place for the signature has a printed 'X' next to it? Well, that's not just a formality or sort of old custom. It's really necessary, because most of the people who have trouble with reading and writing can write their names by rote but they can't read so they don't know where on a form they're supposed to write their names. And these people will sign almost anything rather than admit that they can't read. You should see some of the sales contracts they sign.

"There's another difference it makes to them in the city. They're afraid to leave their own neighborhood. They don't dare ride the buses or the subway trains. It's pretty simple. They can't read directions or the signs on buses or the street signs. If they ask directions, someone's going to say to go as far as Clark Street and turn left, but they won't be able to read 'Clark' on the street sign when they get there. So the parents stick to home and the kids don't get out.

"And it goes deeper than that. You know one of the first things I have to do with my class of adults in reading and writing? Sex education. Not for them. It's too late for that. But the parents don't know any polite terms for parts of the body or for the various sex and other functions. All they know are the vulgar, the gutter words. So they're embarrassed to talk to their kids about it. If the kids ask them a question, the parents get angry and say they're busy. A slum girl has her first menstruation without warning, and when it happens the mother can tell her hardly anything about it because she's humiliated to use the dirty words. They have trouble warning their kids about sex and this neighborhood needs a lot of warning. So I have to get to the blackboard and just put things down straight from the shoulder and write the polite words and speak them and the *class is pretty embarrassed sometimes but they take it all in. Here I'm a kid in college and I'm teaching sex to parents with a dozen kids."*

Sister Mary William strode in and gathered her staff around to monitor a teen-age dance in the upper floor of the settlement house. She sat at a table near the dance floor and watched the couples, her starched white cap turning like a searchlight back and forth. *"Elaine!"* she called and a trim, hard-looking girl came to the table. *"You know the rules,"* Sister Mary William told her brusquely. *"No stretch pants. Next time, out you go."* The girl simpered and went back to the dance floor. *"Fifteen years old,"* the nun said, *"and she's had a baby born out of wedlock."*

Her quick brown eyes conned the couples as she talked and again she broke off with a loud, *"Robert! No contact. No cheek-to-cheek!"* Robert was a gay, ginger-colored boy who pretended alarm and began dancing with exaggerated formality, his partner held at stiff arm's length. Everyone laughed, including the nun. But a moment later she called, *"Robert!"* again as the boy and girl coalesced into a glued tangle. The nun talked some more. In the middle of a sentence she stood up, walked over to the dance floor. Robert began retreating toward a cloak rack. He ducked behind hangers and jackets, but Sister Mary William pushed aside the garments and with a wide swinging open palm smacked the boy so hard his head shook and his face showed the blotch of the blow. *"Once more and you're out of here for good,"* she said. She returned to the table. *"You can't let them get away with an inch. It's like a flood. Once it gets a trickle it will just sweep you away. It may look tough and cruel but you can't equivocate. I get grabbed every now and then in a dark corridor and you've got to convince them you mean business or else they'll go wild. At the same time, you've got to keep their respect. It's like handling dynamite. You just can't turn your back because it'll blow up and you can't just smother it. But you've got to keep it under control. That Robert is a bright kid and he's funny and quick. But when I slapped him he had made an obscene move with the girl. If he had got away with that, there'd be no controlling anyone. You know, when there's nothing else in your life, sex gets to be even bigger than it is in most teenagers.*

"Prostitution? Prostitution in this neighborhood?" She laughed. "*Why, there's not enough money here for prostitution. If you mean promiscuity, there's plenty of that. The girls here are very aggressive, much more so than the boys. They're all jammed in pretty close where they live. No privacy at home. They've grown up seeing and hearing just about everything that goes on with adults and a lot goes on. Not much privacy outside either. No, I'm afraid the girls don't sell themselves: they give themselves. At twelve, thirteen, fourteen . . . The way it happens lots of times is that a kid skips school. He's got no place to go so they get a kid to skip whose mother and father are both working so their flat is empty. So they sit around and play cards and look at TV. Then a little later they skip school and they get someone who can get his hands on some cheap wine. Then they skip for a couple of days and go to one of the empty flats with wine and this time with both boys and girls. After that, school looks pretty tame.*"

The nun called out to another couple, "*Cut the chin-to-chin!*" And said quietly, "*That's a new one. You know,* there's a lot of strange business in a slum like this but the basic problem is pretty simple: they don't have anyone to love them. The families don't and usually the kids don't. I wasn't rich when we grew up in St. Louis. My father was office manager of a laundry and when the Depression came he had his salary cut in half. But we had something. There was still a job. We knew things were going to get better. And we had love. We had the love of the family and the family life that a lot of people take for granted as the ordinary way of living but when it isn't there it means something.

"For example, there's one family in the neighborhood that I managed to get a Thanksgiving dinner for, turkey and the works. So I went to the mother and asked her if she needed any help to get the dinner ready. And you know what? It turned out they weren't going to sit down together because they never had. A lot of families here never have. I asked her why and she said, 'Number One, we ain't got enough chairs. Number Two, we ain't got enough dishes. Number Three, we ain't got enough knives and forks. Number Four, they'd think I was crazy.' Well, I got some dishes and all the rest of the stuff and we got some boxes and borrowed some chairs. And at Thanksgiving we all sat down. It was strange and self-conscious for them. The kids giggled. The mother didn't know what to do. And the father got disgusted and walked out. It was the first time they had ever sat down together at the table as a whole family. But it didn't work. What usually happens with families like that is that the pot with supper in it is done about four or five in the afternoon and the mother or oldest girl has the job of watching to make sure that when each person comes along to take something out of it he takes only his share and doesn't try seconds before everyone has eaten. But they do it one at a time.

"There's another family near them, full of kids where the poor mother just spent every minute from morning to night over a washtub, heating water on the stove, pouring it into the tub, beating the clothes by hand, wringing them out, rinsing, hour after hour. So I arranged to get a donated washing machine. What do you mean, how did I arrange it? I'm Irish and I'm a nun and I know how to put the arm on someone the Good Lord has chosen to donate a washing machine to the poor. So we got a nice new electric washing machine with a roller wringer and had it delivered to the door. What did the mother do? She refused it. She wouldn't let them in the door. They told her it was free but they couldn't get by. I had to talk to her for five minutes and give her my solemn word that there were no strings attached before she'd let it in the house.

"And when you see what happens to these people, she was perfectly right. You have no idea how these people are exploited. They're greenhorns. A lot of them can't read. There's a lot of dirty fraud, of slick guys going door-to-door pretending to be all kinds of things—preachers, welfare workers, anything, leaving something in the house saying it's on free trial and getting a signature and then returning with someone they say is a lawyer to take them into court because they agreed to buy it. Or else they are threatened with jail if they don't fork over $10 a week. Or they threaten to garnishee the father's pay. Or a salesman will show a beautiful sample of something, get a signed order for a delivery, and the next week a piece of junk arrives. So when this woman saw a new machine coming into the house, she wouldn't budge until I talked her into it. But after that, whew, what a difference. You know what her kids did? They got some old wood and made a religious statue out of it, you know, you can tell it's supposed to be a religious statue, and they painted it black somehow and they wrote on it, 'To Sis Mary William.' I've got it in my room."

She rose quickly and went to the corner where the record-player was booming out a feverish number that had the couples in frenzy. "I said that number's out," she announced. The more restrained music of Chubby Checker took its place.

"You see that girl changing the records? She had a grandmother was sick a few months ago. She needed a doctor. The problem of doctors in the slums is very simple. The poor don't have doctors. Sure, I know all that stuff that nobody lacks proper medical attention because they haven't any money. I know. I live here. I'm here twenty-four hours a day. The poor don't have doctors. Period. You can call on the telephone 'til you're blue in the face and no doctor will come out. The minute he hears the address he can't make it. So that girl's grandmother was very old and they came running to me one day and I hotfooted it over there. The old lady was unconscious. It turned out later she had a bladder obstruction. But all we knew was that she had been in terrible pain and they couldn't get a doctor. And then she had passed out. So then they called me. I called doctor after doctor and all the places you might expect to get a doctor. I told them who I was, that an old lady was unconscious. But no soap. I could not get a doctor to come to look at this unconscious woman. I finally got an ambulance from Cook County Hospital. Don't tell me nobody lacks medical care because of his economic status. That's a laugh."

By now the dance was over. The children were drifting out, most of them calling goodby to the nun, except the girl in the stretch pants who walked by sullenly, her head held stiffly.

"I'm afraid for that girl," the nun said. "But if you knew her family life you'd be surprised that she was this civilized. You know, for most of these kids there's no one single thing to hold their lives together. The welfare provides the money for food and housing. The school takes care of some education a few hours a day, but the teachers wait for the bell to ring and shoot out of the neighborhood in their cars. But the poor need people who know them, who are near them, and who can be depended on. That's where we come in. We're the putty in the cracks of their lives."

By now it was after eleven o'clock and the bleak street scenery was broken by circles of light from street lamps, even they picking up the broken glass and the fitful movement of scraps of paper in the wind.

"Even my poor father couldn't understand why I was here, at first. He came from St. Louis after I first started work here. He took one look at the neighborhood and his face got white and he said, 'What did you do wrong that they sent you here?' But he sends me $10 every month for our work. He knows now that what we need here is more than food and doctors and good teachers, although the

Good Lord knows we need plenty of that. But what we
need more than anything else is love."

It was Chicago's poet, Carl Sandburg, who wrote:

> Give me hunger,
> O you gods that sit and give
> The world its orders.
> Give me hunger, pain and want,
> Shut me out with shame and failure
> From your doors of gold and fame,
> Give me your shabbiest, weariest hunger!
>
> But leave me a little love . . .

CHAPTER TWELVE

"They are fierce and smelly . . . helpless and childish."

"The tenants," a report from the building inspector said, "seem to wholly disregard personal cleanliness and the very first principles of decency."

Another described the anti-social behavior of people who "have been drawing their knives on each other today . . . like hungry lions towards everyone else. . . . They are fierce and smelly, as helpless and childish, as dangerous and tricky, as cunning and idolatrous as each other . . ."

Modern slum-dwellers? Ghetto residents? Juvenile delinquents in the cities? Negroes?

The first is a report published in 1864 about a predominantly Irish neighborhood. The second is a letter written by a Welshman in 1844 about German immigrants.

The impoverished newcomer still has the same impact on the established resident. Throughout history the poor have looked about the same to the rich: depraved, dirty, stupid, and untrustworthy, the unchanging and unchangeable fruit of their genes. The rationalization of the comfortable observer has been that Nature protects the poor because the poor, like dissected frogs in the laboratory and live lobsters in boiling water, are endowed with primitive nervous systems and therefore do not suffer as do we sensitive souls.

The poor, in fact, are not often attractive by normal standards of material refinement and social grace. Toward the outside they tend to display intolerance, suspicion, and withdrawal. Among many of the poor there is resistance to improvement, or at least to the kind of improvement conventionally pressed upon them. Their nervous systems are at least as susceptible to pain and fatigue as those of the rest of the human race, but the poor suffer in ways not always understood by remote observers.

The most common error of the comfortable onlooker of the poor is that he is viewing the result of some exclusively individual trait. The poor, indeed, have individual characteristics but they are also the products of a special way of life imposed on them not by their genes alone but by their poverty. There is a culture of poverty that perpetuates itself inside its own geography behind a border that separates the despairing from the hopeful. It provides an enclave for refugees from the world of success. These duchies of deprivation are running blots throughout the national landscape. From the outside, the inhabitants seem hostile and irrational. But from within, the culture is sensible and inevitable and has the positive profit of drawing from morbid circumstance the warmest possible human qualities.

The characteristics of the poor as seen from the outside are real enough: apathy, hopelessness, bewilderment with the outside world, retreat. The root is frustration, a bitter bafflement with the larger world. The poor in the United States, like the affluent, are constantly provoked by messages to succeed, to work, to save, to spend, to rise. These signals come from all sides and from all authority, from school, from church, from television, from billboards, from the personal delegations of the outer kingdom. The affluent have found some measure of satisfactory response to these signals, so to them the stimulus makes sense; achievement, being common among them, appears to be an unlimited possibility for as many as wish to seize it.

But the poor have not been able to find a good answer to these proddings, or if they once did they have now lost it. Among them it is rare to find material success; achievement, being rare, strikes them as a scarce commodity without enough for all. So, to the poor, the go-getter is calloused and self-centered; the man who competes fiercely is anti-social and disloyal to his friends. He is, after all, turning his back on people in order to grab for himself the tiny portion of success available to the group. Denied the fruits of ambition in an ambitious, Calvinistic society, the poor abjure ambition and thus alienate themselves from the standards of their own country. Contact with the middle-class world is almost always an occasion for embarrassment or humiliation, so the poor retreat. The slum child eager to answer the teacher's questions in school is considered a lackey willing to make his friends look bad in order to curry favor with "her." Friends, after all, are more important than a career—especially if there is no career.

The culture of poverty downgrades the male, for the man who does not work loses some of his manliness. In many families the man not only stays home, but the wife then goes to work at the marginal jobs available to women and not to men. The household role of father and mother is reversed, with profound effects on the whole family. Millions of slum children never ask their fathers for money or advice or help, but instead go to their mothers who have the paycheck or welfare money. It is not surprising to find slum girls aggressive and slum boys unusually dependent upon groups rather than upon themselves.

In such a world, the old standards turn on themselves. It is possible to watch men like Willie Johnson in West Virginia, who grew up in a world where hard work was the only manly course in life, grow apathetic and defeated. His old standards are intolerable. For one thing, there are no jobs but somehow he must find a tolerable self-acceptance though he does not work. For another, he has to reject the old standards to accept welfare that keeps his family alive. Throughout the depressed areas, the will to work deteriorates, the dependency on free food and shelter becomes a way of life that must be made acceptable, though once they were unacceptable. Edmund MacIntosh, pale and weak on his bed in the miserable Los Angeles hotel, was still bewildered in the shift from self-reliance to welfare. *"Now, welfare, that's charity and something else. But Social Security, that's yours, you work for that yourself . . ."* It is a positive and good belief. But Edmund MacIntosh was old, alone, sick, his bank account about gone. He would soon find himself rejecting his old standards, unless, of course, he rejected life itself.

Much of the culture of poverty makes life emotionally tolerable, but much of it also cripples the ability to re-enter the world of achievement. Tragically, a great deal done by the outside world reinforces the most harmful emotions of the poor.

Social welfare practices in the United States tend to deepen the culture of poverty, not dissipate it, to thrust the recipient of aid further from society, not bring him closer. They let the recipient know he is considered an inherent cheater, by an obsessive and unrealistic concern with small infractions. Society has a legitimate concern with how its welfare money is spent but there is something unhealthy in the passion for spying on the poor. It may be natural that workers in welfare systems become impatient but the barking clerks, the calloused bureaucracy, and the absence of civility become, with the poor, more than unpleasant procedures. They poison the precise area where the poor might maintain a hope of clinging to the larger world.

Even the machinery of justice has a double standard. There is, according to the National Social Welfare Assembly, "a growing disposition in some states and localities to apply a different standard of law enforcement to persons *because* of their poverty, especially if that poverty is reflected in dependence upon tax-supported benefits such as public assistance."

It would be unthinkable, for example, that an American mother would have her children taken from her by the state because she is visited by a male friend, or that anyone would enter her home without a warrant and search her closets and refrigerator. But this is common with welfare recipients, though such acts are probably unconstitutional. The poor have few friends in court and are not in a position to protest.

There is something wrong when something like this occurs (as it did in Chicago):

An unemployed man on relief heard of a job on the other side of the city. The welfare worker agreed he should apply and gave him two bus tokens for the trip to the plant. Then the welfare worker—a college graduate with a large caseload of families to supervise—shadowed the man to make sure he did not swap the tokens for a package of cigarettes and then walk to his appointment. The welfare recipient knew he was being followed and why.

It is not unusual to have social workers arrive at a house in pairs, one entering by the front door and one by the rear, to conduct a systematic search for (1) an adult male, or (2) contraband clothes and food. In some cases the search for a male is demanded by a rule against welfare to families with a healthy adult male, causing some fathers to abandon their families and sneak back to visit on occasion. Or it may be an attempt to catch an unattached mother with a boy friend in the official hope of preventing illegitimate children and/or gifts of clothing and food which the mother might not report to the welfare department.

The official reason for such searches and surveillance is to prevent wasting of welfare money on families who have some other source of income. The real reason is the cruel exploitation of welfare in politics. The poor seldom have effective representation in city councils, county governments, state legislatures, or in Congress. There is constant agitation in politics, often stimulated and abetted by newspapers, to get "welfare chiselers," with the implication that there is something inherently dishonest among all welfare recipients and that existing violations of rules are significant. There are widespread technical infractions in the sense that a large number of welfare recipients receive small additions of food and clothing which they do not report—a child collects and cashes in empty bottles, a relative gives an old overcoat, an older girl baby-sits. Neither in the proportion of welfare money that is involved nor in the allocation of time and energy by staffs do these petty events justify the obsessive injustice constantly visited upon all welfare recipients. In the broadest study yet done of a major program, aid to dependent children, the Institute for Research in Social Science of the University of North Carolina found in forty-two states and the District of Columbia that one-third of cases closed still left the family in need of help (81 per cent of children were legitimate and 50 per cent of cases had received assistance less than eighteen months).

The pressure on social welfare departments to cut budgets is constant. During newspaper agitation or political attacks it becomes unbearable and welfare supervisors sometimes hand down a quota to each worker to cut individuals off the rolls. The best social workers refuse this arbitrary and cruel withdrawal of food and clothing, but for this they pay by the disfavor that comes from failure to cooperate with a superior protecting his own domain. The conscientious social worker may find herself unpromoted because she has not cut her budget.

The long-range folly of such campaigns is evident from this very real and not rare case:

A family on welfare consisted of a father disabled by bone cancer, a mother, and six children, the youngest one year, the oldest fifteen years. The oldest boy had hinted that maybe he could get a job when he was sixteen but the family halfheartedly demurred. A job is such a dazzling achievement it is a constant temptation to most welfare families to search one out. The social worker in three successive visits remarked, *"Let's see, Junior will be sixteen in a couple of months won't he?"* and again, *"What does Junior say about working papers when he gets to be sixteen?"* The family, including Junior, did not need much more encouragement. Junior at age sixteen dropped out of school and looked for work. The welfare worker was able to report an individual dropped off the roll, with a budget reduction in prospect. Junior looked diligently and found that the best he could do was work at a carwash stand on weekends for $30. This was heady income for an impoverished boy of sixteen and it made a splendid budgetary drop in the family welfare check. But Junior, of course, did not go beyond the tenth grade, he had no long-range employable skills and the odds are high that he will become an endemic welfare case, along with his own family, for years to come. But that will be someone else's worry, to be worked on during some other intense campaign to cut the welfare budget.

The disproportionate time spent on detective work by trained social workers is directed toward finding an excuse for cutting the budget, but it is sometimes abetted by a personal impulse in the field worker. Social workers are not infrequently career women from middle-class backgrounds, usually unmarried. Often there runs a sense of puritanical retribution toward the female welfare recipient who is enjoying sex.

The irony of budget-cutting blitzkriegs is that they deepen dependency and perpetuate poverty. They penalize enterprise. They multiply welfare cases by failing to save the children who, unmotivated, poorly educated, untrained, enter adult lives unable to keep up in a white collar, technical world of jobs.

The cruelty of most attacks on welfare is their cynicism. In Illinois a political struggle in the legislature sent starving families onto the sidewalks for food. In Newburgh, New York, a city manager ideologically opposed to the idea of welfare imposed rules supposedly to force recipients to go "back to work"—when jobs demonstrably did not exist. In Washington, D. C., a family with an unemployed able-bodied father at home cannot get welfare aid, nor can a family whose breadwinner is being trained for a new job. These families are forbidden help at the insistence of Senator Robert C. Byrd of West Virginia who rules the congressional committee controlling the District's money. The cynicism seems plain enough: in Senator Byrd's own West Virginia both programs—aid to families with a father living at home and to families whose breadwinner is training for a new job—are integral parts of the state's welfare program, with no complaint by Senator Byrd. But the Senator gets considerable sympathy and support from Southern members of Congress who know that most of Washington's welfare families are Negro.

Even at its most compassionate, the world of affluence has an irrepressible desire to make the poor act like middle-class white collar folk. The nuns in an Arizona Indian mission had painfully taught teen-age Papagos girls to dance the minuet and the girls, their dark braids tucked under Restoration costume hats, moved woodenly through their steps, their faces expressionless, their bodies lugubrious. Minutes later in their own Rain Dance, eyes flashed, feet flicked in time and faces rose in animation. In a Chicago settlement house, a worker tried to teach Negro teen-age slum children square dancing, the children alternating between listless obedience and collapse in laughter and disgust. When they were permitted to dance the Limbo, life was real again. Middle-class mores aren't that easy; they come from a way of life. So do the mores of the poor.

The poor are not automatons. They are individuals with their own family and cultural traditions, with much to offer to surrounding society. The American culture is an amalgam of many elements once ignored or despised by the larger society. The imposition of a bland, homogenized middle-class culture robs both the poor and the affluent.

There is nothing new in the attitude of the comfortable toward the poor, nor in the poor's view of the outside world. This has been constant in history, existing in the United States while millions of people moved out of the sub-culture of poverty into self-sufficiency and productive lives. Yet there are some reasons for worry today. The Negro, for the first time in the history of minorities in the United States, is becoming permanently frozen into the slums. "Structural unemployment," the extended joblessness of workers willing and able to do modern labor, has been with us for over a decade despite general prosperity. There is an ominous pattern of large groups of the dispossessed who, with modern communications to see the relative misery of their position, have been willing to smash the machinery of comfortable society rather than endure their status.

So it is not enough to say that in the 1860's the affluent thought the poor "helpless and childish" and were wrong; and that in the 1960's this continues to be true. Today the swiftness of political reaction has something of the acceleration of television over the carrier pigeon. The United States has had a unique and powerful experience with the dispossessed but it seems now to have forgotten it. The native observers thought the Irish and German immigrants a century ago to be animal-like, yet two generations later these same Irish and Germans had become the most highly integrated minorities in the American culture and their children and grandchildren became the nation's political and business leaders. With success, many of these grandchildren adopted the same attitude toward newcomers that native Americans had imposed on the early Irish and Germans. There is a continuing history of native Americans looking down on the disgusting poverty of the newly arrived Germans who in the next generation looked down on the newly arrived Irish who in the next generation looked down on the newly arrived Italians who in the next generation looked down on the newly migrated Negroes, each ascribing the condition of the newcomer to some unchangeable ethnic way of life. This is one proof that the culture of poverty may remain essentially unchanged while under the right circumstances individuals are quick to extricate themselves from it. And it is dismal proof that memories of the affluent are short.

"... he who desires more ... is poor."

What is "poor" in the United States in the 1960's?

Charlemagne, Emperor of the West, had no flush toilet. No central heating warmed him. If he caught pneumonia he had no medicine to shift the odds in his favor. He died, as a matter of fact, of pleurisy.

John Jacob Astor, the richest man in America when he died over a century ago, had barely any education, never could write very well, and of his eight children three died while very young.

Most of the American poor in the 1960's are better off in some important ways than the most powerful man in Europe in the ninth century and the richest in America in the first half of the nineteenth. Almost no one dies of pleurisy any more. And if a family loses three children out of eight it is considered a fantastic tragedy or cause for investigation. But neither poverty nor wealth have been constants through the years. They are both judged within a man's own community by the standards of his own time.

Poverty involves comparisons with others and it is the comparison that produces the sense of failure. Yet poverty is more than just a state of mind. The modern American is not competing with Charlemagne or John Jacob Astor, but with the generality of men in his own time. In the 1960's when a father enters an employment agency he will not be judged on how he compares with ancient kings but on how well he reads a blueprint; when his child sets goals in life they will depend not on their relevance to the life of Astor but on how competent the child is in English composition.

The power of comparisons has been multiplied with rapid communications and this has made the impact of poverty a new force in society. The concentration of men in cities plus the common instruments of seeing and hearing the conditions of others has broadened the consciousness of human identity. If men were ever content to endure the morbidities of the past—most of the young dying in infancy, the diseased remaining crippled for life, the survivors spending all their waking hours in the struggle for food and shelter—they are not content today. With access to printing, to cosmopolitan teachers, to radio and television, the poor see a world in which all men do not lose their children to malnutrition or spend their lives in fruitless toil. What was once an unalterable condition of life has now been accepted as alterable. The Roman philosopher Seneca said, "It is not the man who has little, but he who desires more, that is poor." Seneca, of course, was quite right (and quite rich). He implies that poverty is perpetual and only envy causes agitation for change. If it were ever the case that the poor did not expect to improve themselves, this time has passed; the placidity of the dispossessed rested upon isolation and silence which are no more. The poor and the rich can no longer ignore each other.

The easiest way of comparing the affluence of various persons is by counting cash. This does not describe a man's worth as a human being or the richness of his life. But in a modern cash economy it is justified as a measure because below a certain level of material wealth a man loses the ability to participate in his own civilization. Lack of money, contrary to romantic notions, is more likely to destroy peace than produce it: it is not wise to idealize the emotional effects of a man worrying about how to feed his children.

To be sure, counting cash has its obvious disadvantages in describing a way of life. There are slum-dwellers— dishwashers or hospital workers or welfare recipients—who are incomparably more depressed on $2400 a year than farm families on $1500. There are aging couples, alone and transfixed by increasing illness, who are more tragic on $2000 a year than a young graduate student and his wife, filled with vigor and hope, living in a garret on $1400. It is also true that some people use money more wisely than others, that cash goes further in some places, and individuals vary greatly in their ability to cope with adversity. But money is still the most reliable measure of poverty in the mass.

The average family income in the United States during 1960 was $6845. If poverty involves a comparison with the general standard, certainly "average" is not poor. But "average" is an abstraction. If the owner of a mansion has an annual income of $500,000 and the families of his four servants have incomes of $2000 a year each, the average family income for that block is $101,600, which tells nothing about any particular family's income. Thus, though the average American family has $6845 a year, half of all families have less than $5600; one-third have less than $4000;

22 per cent less than $3000; and 13 per cent less than $2000.

Fixing the dollar level of poverty—the point at which a person is seriously short of minimal food, shelter, and medical care—cannot be done precisely. Men disagree on what is "minimal." Basic needs vary from family to family and region to region. There is a great deal that is not known about income, living conditions, and nutrition. Size of family plainly makes a difference on the impact of a given income, though using a four-member family as an average brings the same total result as calculations of the money needs for each size of family. The best that can be done is to find the income range of poverty.

In 1959 the Department of Labor surveyed twenty American cities to determine a "modest but adequate" family budget. This varied from city to city ($5421 in Houston; $6629 in Chicago) with many cities clustered around $6000. "Modest but adequate" is not poor. At least it is clear that poverty is somewhere below $6000. In the typical "modest but adequate" income for a family of four, the basic food, shelter, medical care, taxes, and irreducible work expense comes to about $4000. Yet at $4000 the family has not yet paid for clothes, education, recreation, household equipment, or savings for emergencies. Thus, at some point around $4000 a family of four is in danger of losing its grip on basic needs that cannot be postponed.

By some calculations, $4000 is already a state of poverty. The Health and Welfare Council, Inc., of Philadelphia, estimates that a family with less than $4600 a year cannot afford ordinary medical and dental care. In the

1930's, the Works Progress Administration calculated that 70 per cent of an "adequate" family budget was tolerable as a short-term emergency but would be permanently injurious to health if maintained for a long time; 70 per cent of the "adequate" $6000 budget of 1959 is $4200.

For lone individuals, the Bureau of Labor Statistics regards $1500 as necessary to live modestly. Individuals suffer more per dollar loss from this level than families: one man loses proportionately more food to the cooking utensils than a family of four, he pays more for food because he buys in smaller quantities, and he has no built-in system of hand-me-downs in clothing or the mutual assistance of a household group.

It would seem safe to assume that a family with $3000 annual income or an individual with $1000 is poor. Within the range of a few hundred dollars, all such numbers are arbitrary. The uncertainty is increased by the fact that some statistics on "adequate" income include non-cash items like free rent and food, while others refer to cash alone. But on either statistical basis—despite variations of a few hundred dollars in basic needs and discrepancies between cash and non-cash incomes—the totals are not arbitrary because in both cases a large number of human beings is involved. The precise number is arguable. The massive suffering is not.

If lone persons with less than $1000 cash income and families with less than $3000 are poor, there are 36,000,000 impoverished Americans, or 20 per cent of the population.

Use different incomes for poverty and the numbers of

people involved are still substantial. At the very least—and it would be hard to imagine anyone arguing with this income as meaning poverty—11 per cent of men, women, and children in the country are poor. Using a higher figure, 30 per cent are poor. For example, assuming a total population of approximately 180,000,000, we have:

11%	20,000,000—individuals with less than $500; families with less than $2000.
15%	27,500,000—individuals, $500; families, $2500.
16%	29,500,000—individuals, $1000; families, $2500.
20%	36,000,000—individuals, $1000; families, $3000.
25%	45,500,000—individuals, $1500; families, $3500.
30%	54,000,000—individuals, $2000; families, $4000.

Whether there are 20,000,000 poor or 54,000,000, either represents more degradation, suffering, and social blight than the American ethic can tolerate.

Who are these poor? They are not easily separated and counted. There are about 8,000,000 in rural areas, but some of these are also among the 8,000,000 aged poor. About 7,000,000 are "unskilled" workers. About half are in households where a man is out of work. Many others are dependent on wages that can't raise the family out of poverty. Interspersed among these are the semi-permanently unemployed, the coal miners, steel workers, meat cutters, auto workers, families of men who once worked for the most respectable wages in American industry but who for years have been replaced by machinery and have been drifting downward in the economy and social structure until they are now poor. There are special groups—the 500,000 American Indians and the few hundred thousand derelicts of Skid Row—who are small in proportion of the whole but appalling in the total individual tragedy.

Most notable today is the Negro, once concentrated in the rural South but now two-thirds in the cities, North and South. Many made the move during World War II and the Korean War when urgent national need overcame some race prejudice in jobs, a time when 14 per cent of all Negroes in the country moved to a different state. But when recession and automation came, the Negroes, last to be hired, were the first to be fired. Their bitterness is all the more deep for having been partially engaged with the larger society and then dropped by it. The Negro unemployment rate is twice that of whites; those who do work get 7 per cent fewer hours and 40 per cent lower wages. Regardless of their income, the vast majority of Negroes are excluded from the normal housing market, the primary benefit for most American families who improve their wages.

But poverty is not limited to Negroes. One calculation shows Negroes to constitute 22 per cent of the poor, double their proportion of the population, but with whites still constituting the great majority. It is fashionable to argue that almost all the American poor are unemployable —they have personal failings that seriously inhibit their usefulness in society. There are, of course, some individuals whose poverty is caused primarily by their own disabilities —they are blind or mute or deaf, they are otherwise physically disabled, they are of extremely low intelligence, they are emotionally disturbed. But what statistics are known do not suggest that this explains away poverty in the

United States. And there is reason to believe that a great many Americans in productive life have the same characteristics of the so-called "unemployables" but by luck and constructive social circumstance they entered the normal life of work and this strengthened their capacity for overcoming weaknesses. The Conference on Economic Progress estimates these characteristics of the poor (the categories overlap, and so add up to more than 100 per cent): 57 per cent are in households whose heads had eight years or less education; 43 per cent live in the South; 31 per cent are headed by a female; 28 per cent are unemployed; 23 per cent are over 65; 22 per cent are non-white; and 17 per cent live on farms.

There is one characteristic of the poor that the United States ignores at its peril:

In the families of the poor there are 12,000,000 children. These are the hostages to poverty. They and millions of underemployed young adults are an important segment of the next generation of national life. They represent a future multiplication of misery. They have inherited a bleak and hopeless outlook which for most of them already has poisoned the education that could save them. They are destined to enlarge despair as an ingredient in the life of the nation unless some way can be found to break their unhappy legacy.

It is considered sound to argue for the salvation of the poor on grounds that it will save money in the long run. This is a valid argument. It will save money. But there is something wrong in the national habit of arguing social betterment almost exclusively on the basis that it will show a dollars-and-cents profit. The poor suffer disease and estrangement beyond their share as fellow human beings. Most of this is preventable to begin with and repairable afterward. A civilized country should not have to apologize for wanting to help the economically paralyzed any more than it does for the care of crippled children or of men found dying in the streets. The United States has a history of decent concern with the suffering of others. But it has become so frightened of the sound of any social doctrine contrary to legendary laissez faire that in the world of conventional commerce and in legislative bodies it has become disreputable to use national wealth to end national poverty unless it can be justified as financially profitable. Needless to say, there is energy and money put to good social purpose without expectation of immediate or provable return—in medical research, welfare funds, education —but it is far too small in relation to national wealth and need, and when under fire it is usually defended as necessary to keep business healthy and happy. For it is considered unbusinesslike and unbusinessmanlike to spend national money merely for the non-fiscal betterment of personal life.

The commercial community has a fundamental hostility toward social welfare programs which is ironic, indeed.

The mixed economy of the United States works, for one thing, because some socialistic devices have been used to prevent the dissolution of all business enterprise. These devices have been applied with ingenuity and imagination to the special requirements of the American people and have, for over a generation, prevented the collapse of a system of individual free choice and have permitted the growth of private, if mostly large, business enterprise. Yet these saving social devices carry a stigma that hampers their open and rational application to new problems. They continue to be attacked regularly as inimicable to private enterprise, apparently to be left in American political limbo until there is a catastrophic collapse of the economy, as in the Great Depression, and the business community is faced with truly rigid doctrine. It is time to accept the legitimacy and need of welfare programs where there is no effective humane alternative.

But this legitimacy is still clouded in the official mythology. Social security, unemployment compensation, and other social insurance programs continue to be attacked as socialism, creeping and galloping, and infused with guilt rather than pride. All over the world the United States argues for its values as a government and as a system of human association. The major argument against the American method is that while the United States is rich it offers the ordinary citizen no security in his job or old age and that "the American way of life" is really "dog-eat-dog." This is nonsense, but in one form or another this nonsense is widely believed. For most of this, the United States has itself to blame. It has, through its sacred political mythology, been robbed of an understandable vocabulary to describe itself.

The greatest loss from this refusal to acknowledge the true value of social welfare is not in any debate with foreigners. The loss is to Americans themselves. The country desperately needs a creative dialogue on social welfare and economics, carried on in realistic language without the noisy incantations of political demonology.

The need for this dialogue and some sensible conse-
quence of it is urgent. Ordinary welfare programs are inadequate, and do poorly even with their lightest of loads.
In addition, there is a new stress on the economy from a
fast-moving technology and a mobile, growing population.
Whole industries die and are replaced by new ones in a
few years, in a small portion of one man's working career.
Large factories move from one coast to another. But these
are not neat equations with new jobs and displaced workers in never-ending balance. There are always a sizeable
number of men, women, and children whose food and
shelter, through no fault of their own, has suddenly been
withdrawn. It was no sloth on the part of the coal miner
that caused petroleum to emerge as the more versatile fuel.
It was no weakness in the railroad engineer that made the
car and truck dominate transportation. Nor was it because farmers worked less hard that expensive machinery
became more profitable than the simple plow. The American system is productive and is competitive with those
abroad because it is able to change; these changes mean
that at any given time a large number of families will face
starvation unless something intervenes and a mass of
once-employable men will become obsolete human beings
while still in the prime of life. Yet, the politics and social
values of the commercial community, which depend on
this versatility and change, assume that poverty and unemployment are casual, self-imposed and self-liquidating.
It remains almost impossible to pass national legislation
to take even elementary steps to solve the greatest single
blight threatening the commercial community.

One irony of this is that if Social Security and social

welfare payments were stopped today there would be chaos and terror within a matter of weeks. Men, women, and children no longer starve quietly, if they ever did. The stability and moderation so desired by private enterprise could not last three months without the social devices the commercial community is prone to call un-American.

The other irony is that social welfare programs as they exist today need intelligent criticism. They are at least as susceptible to waste and error as other human enterprises. But the most common critics seldom address themselves to the basic waste—the failure to return more welfare recipients to productive life. Some acknowledge this failure but suggest only that welfare be cut off to force people back to work—but almost never concern themselves with how this happy end result will come about. These critics are seldom found seriously looking for an end to the appalling loss of human resources that comes when large numbers of citizens are kept below the threshold of participation in the economy as customer and producer. Instead, the conventional criticism of welfare programs is directed at the woman who does a day's housework without reporting it, the bus token exchanged for a pack of cigarettes, the unreported dress from a boy friend, and the most grotesque of all welfare criticisms, the feeding of infants who have no certified father. Compared to the fundamental waste in present social welfare practices, these losses on which most energy is expended, are ridiculous. The kind of welfare "cheating" most often found in newspaper campaigns and legislative fulminations is minute in terms of dollars lost or in proportion to all welfare appropriations but it has a sorry fascination for the thoughtless. The wel-

fare political racket, the exploitation of the system for pub-
licity or ideological purposes while ignoring the lives of the
men, women, and children involved, is the closest the
United States comes to the habitual bullying of defenseless
citizens. The poor are a safe target. They can't hit back.

The energy spent on this unadmirable pastime would
be better spent on serious alterations of the basic system,
done by men devoted to solving the human problems. The
advance of computers and automatic machinery will ac-
celerate obsolescence of the present generation of work-
ingmen. The welfare problem will get deeper and more
complicated. It is doubtful that there is validity in the old
assurance that new machines create more jobs than they
eliminate. "I am not sure it is right," Willard Wirtz, Secre-
tary of Labor, has said. Central to the solution of the automation dilemma will be a decision whether the prosperous
segments of society ought to reinvest in the impoverished.

Among the basic changes needed is recognition that
money alone is not enough. After World War II the United
States made a disturbing discovery. It is relatively simple
to destroy a city: all you need is its latitude and longitude.
To help intelligently is far more difficult: it requires an
enormous amount of knowledge and talented insight.
Merely pressing cash upon an ailing society does not work
and often deepens its problem. This is not because cash
has no use but because cash alone is no automatic remedy.
It is not so different with individuals.

The poor in the United States have been catapulted
into a new culture they cannot grasp or they have drifted
out of contact with the working world. Money is needed to
keep them alive and healthy. But something more is

needed. The greatest gap between the poor and the affluent in the United States is not $7000 per family but the
lack of human beings who bridge the two worlds. This is
not an easy bridge to build. It is not enough to be well-
versed in the world of comfort and carry this knowledge to
the poor as a kind of rich man's burden. It is more pertinent to be well-versed in the world of poverty and to understand the needs and feelings of its victims.

If the city is, as Le Corbusier says, a machine, it is one
that frustrates and enrages even its successful children. The
rural person is confronted with learning at once what Urban Man has accumulated in knowledge for centuries.
What the impoverished and innocent newcomers need,
among other things, is a reliable clearing house about city
life. Not a bureaucratic clearing house or welfare pamphlet
or even a low-income Welcome Wagon, though these are
better than nothing. What is needed is a person whose face,
mind, and sympathies are known and trusted. There are
city laws, household practices, shopping places, educational requirements, public health facilities, employment
agencies, recreational possibilities that need to be sorted
out and learned. There are not enough facilities in the great
cities for their contemporary immigrants but there are more
than the newcomers are using.

Children of the slums desperately need tutoring and
individual attention. Nothing in the usual background and
training of the American schoolteacher prepares her for the
special problem of the slum child. Nothing in the background of the child prepares him for the teacher. They are
strangers to each other, commanded by law to be mutually
present a certain number of hours a day, but they part,

usually, still strangers and even bitter enemies. When by chance there is established the communication needed to teach and learn, it is a tenuous line easily broken unless it extends into the home. For lack of this even the most talented teachers have sometimes failed.

In the attack on poverty, education cannot be limited to the children. About half of all heads of poor families barely finished elementary school. Their median years completed is less than 8.8 grades. This is their greatest single drawback to moving into satisfactory jobs, to developing into competent city dwellers, and to promoting their children's education. These adults need further education adapted to their age and circumstance, and for the most part there are no effective programs to give it to them. They need to read and write with greater skill so that they can enter the white collar language in which is found the key to contemporary prosperity. Competence in the culture of paper and words is far more crucial in the 1960's than in the 1900's when foreign immigrants filled the slums.

There is as yet no effective program for matching available jobs to available people. There may be as many as one million jobs open but unfilled, either because men are not trained for the jobs or the trained men live in the wrong places. There is something nonsensical about the common experience in a nation of household machines to be unable to find competent repairmen of household machines even at a physician's hourly rate, yet millions are unemployed. Present government programs plan to train 400,000 men in three years; if this is done it still will not have changed the skills of 90 per cent of the unemployed.

Even when a man has the skills and a job exists for

him in his own community, the man and the job may never meet. The folklore is that most men get new jobs by answering want ads, registering at employment agencies, or bravely applying in person or by letter at all possible places. There is some reason to doubt that this is true. In 1956 the Packard Motor Company closed its doors permanently and threw 4000 men out of work. One study showed that of the men who got new jobs on their own, 75 per cent did it through tips from friends and neighbors. The poor are surrounded by friends and neighbors who, like themselves, have lost communication with the working world.

Today social workers cannot and do not fill the place of knowing friends and neighbors. Usually they can do little but maintain bookkeeping and conduct periodic inspections. They are under enormous pressures to spend their time saving money and detecting infractions of rules. They are not often selected and trained in a way that prepares them for close and sympathetic contact with the ugliness of the slums and the special psychology of the poor. There are among social workers in the United States dedicated men and women of skill and compassion, but for too many in this highly professionalized occupation it is a bureaucratic relationship of superior-and-client.

The best work that is done among the poor is by men and women who live with the poor and have some personal bond with them. This takes a special kind of person and a serious commitment. The most notable of these successes have been related to religion, yet often those who devote their lives to the slums do so out of a strong denominational or fundamentalist feeling that is admirable in its dedication but by its particular orientation limits its ap-

peal. What is needed is a stimulation of the national con-
science to convince more people that this is a cause worth
devoting part of one's life to. This suggests something like
"the domestic Peace Corp" proposed to Congress by President Kennedy. There are slums all over the country awaiting the kind of skilled, dedicated and mature men and
women the international Peace Corps has succeeded in
finding. There is precedent for applying such a corps to
urban life; Puerto Rico has found that the County Agent
system of bringing friendly expertise to the farmer works
well in helping slum-dwellers. A national effort to bridge
the chasm between despair and hope, using the sentiment
of human sympathy but not the sentimentality of *noblesse
oblige*, employing competent men and women to work in-
tensively with people in the rural and urban slums, could
become the greatest single act for overcoming self-perpetu-
ating poverty since enactment of Social Security.

The problem of poverty may remind contemporary
America of a simple truth: he who wishes to live in a civilized community must take responsibility for more than
himself. This is why the childless couple has a stake in the
public schools. People who for years have ignored wretched
schools and miserable slums are too late when they complain bitterly that their towns are unpleasant places to live
in. For if modern urban life has brought men close together it has also given them special powers to influence the
making of their fellow residents.

When it comes to the problems of the poor, the individual American has peculiar responsibility and power.
He has responsibility on general human grounds, but these
are reinforced by the country's tradition of mutual help

and its rejection of the dogma—if not always the practice
—of each class unto itself. It is further intensified by the
fact that in the United States two of the immediate weap-
ons against poverty, social welfare and education, are controlled to an extraordinary degree by local officials. The
Federal government provides most of the money for welfare aid, for example, but the administration of this money
is by local rules and officials. This provides the citizen with
unusual power, for he is faced not with a remote adminis-
trator who can safely ignore the sentiments of a single
town but instead with a man in his own community, ap-
pointed by an official the citizen himself votes for. If there
is little serious pressure for a constructive program for the
poor it is not because the machinery for reform is lacking.
The machinery is uniquely at hand within the United
States; the human beings to use this machinery are merely
asleep.

The local citizen who is affluent has a disproportionate influence in City Hall which rightly suspects the citizen
with money of having better than average skill at bringing
political pressure. And so the affluent citizen has a disproportionate responsibility to use this influence for the good
of his community, to the pragmatic benefit of his own
peace of mind. Let him insist that slum schools be more
than just low-class ordinary schools, aware that to educate
slum children takes at least as much money as to educate
students from college-degree homes. The slums need good
school buildings and specially trained teachers with unusual talents, but the urge to provide them must come
from outside the slums.

The disgrace of American vocational schools must be

ended. In a nation of machines it is difficult to find men competent to maintain machines, yet more than 4,000,000 citizens are unemployed. Our technology is in a computerized, automated, transistorized age but our vocational schools are dusty museums of the nineteenth century. Here, too, the individual citizen has unusual powers. The Federal government is providing increasing help for vocational training but the intelligent and effective use of this money is almost entirely a local matter.

Adult education is desperately needed and our school buildings are empty most of the evenings, yet there are only meager programs to bring the elementary skills of modern life to millions of the poor.

The wrecking ball and bulldozer are on a compulsive rampage throughout the land but they can be controlled if the local hand wills it. All over the country whole neighborhoods are being wiped out in slum clearance and urban renewal and in many cases it is good riddance. But slum clearance seldom means better homes for the poor. It means a more profitable use of the land for parking lots or office buildings or shopping centers or expensive apartments. The old residents simply disappear, to make new slums elsewhere. This, too, is under the influence of the local voter who can, if he will, act soon enough to make sure that slum clearance is not merely a project for getting the poor further out of sight.

In both these areas—creation of schools for children presently untouched by learning, and the building of low-income homes in neighborhoods hospitable to the human spirit—there is much the individual citizen can do in his own community. The United States, unlike most modern countries, leaves these matters to local control. But there is something deeper still. The tradition for personal, voluntary help for the unfortunate is strong in the United States but somehow it has failed to reach the modern poor, perhaps because it is now organized by government on a large scale. Humanitarianism isn't practiced so much as administered. Those hostile to enlargement of government function blame the impersonality of modern "charity" on the intrusion of government. But this intrusion is inevitable. Only tax dollars can provide the food and shelter that keeps an unemployed family alive. It is not the tax dollar that is at fault; it is the taxpayer who thinks the dollar is enough. The human heart is still the chief instrument of salvation for those exiled from the larger world. The best hope for the poor comes from institutions and programs and within them helping hands from the world of achievement. The poor need reliable people who are both compassionate and competent, who are moved by the needs of individuals but who also know how to move City Hall. What the League of Women Voters has done for forgotten political issues, some new community group needs to do for the forgotten poor.

Help for the individual cannot exist in a national vacuum. If men, women and children are to leave poverty, there must be someplace for them to go. The jobless need jobs and today there are not enough jobs. The slum-dwellers need decent homes and today there are not enough decent homes. The uneducated need learning and there is not enough learning. There have not been enough of these things for many years. One reason is the slow rate of growth in the economy which has failed to keep up with the growth in population and the displacement of men by machines.

But a faster rate of growth is not enough. More production could still fail to reach the poor. The United States already is embarrassed by a surplus of food and goods, and yet it has 36,000,000 people who do not have enough food and goods. The problem is a social and political one among the affluent: will we use national energy, including Federal and local government budgets, to provide useful work when private enterprise cannot? Will we invest in the institutions of education and training required to keep our population from being outrun by their machines? The United States has to decide for what purpose its economy works, whether primarily to make bigger and better machines, or to make available to every citizen who wants it an opportunity to work and to pass on to his children a reasonable hope for a full life. The decision cannot be made with vague sentiment. It must be made looking at the mass of men, women, and children who today and for too many years have been suffering deprivation and despair. The answer cannot be comfortable clichés or ideological reflexes, but concrete and immediate proposals made not alone in the living room and learned journal but in our national political dialogue and our legislative chambers. The idle men, the hungry children, the sickly aged have to be at the heart of the decision, not at the periphery.

"*Poverty in the midst of plenty,*" President Kennedy wrote, "*is a paradox that must not go unchallenged.*"

The challenge is not just to help those in need. The poor do indeed need help and in this the rest of the country has a certain self-interest. Poverty is not just the blind guitar player on whom we can look as a rare accident who has our sympathy and our dimes. It is someone much more like ourselves than we would like to believe. But the challenge is to something even deeper. It is to preserve a sense of decency among affluent Americans and to perpetuate what has been the noblest strain in the national ethic.

Author's Notes

CHAPTER ONE (pages 1–9)

Material about the person referred to as "Mrs. Rebecca Franklin" is from a personal interview by the author.

Unemployment in 1962 was 5.6 per cent of the labor force plus 2,700,000 persons who wanted full-time work and could find only part-time jobs. "The total lost was 6.7 per cent of the potential available worktime." *Manpower Report of The President*, March, 1963, p. xiv.

For basis of calculation of the number of poor see notes for Chapter Thirteen.

CHAPTER TWO (pages 10–28)

Data on immigration to Chicago are from Dr. John Hobgood and Mrs. Margaret Madden, of the Chicago Commission on Human Relations.

Episodes on pages 11 and 12 were either heard and witnessed by the author or recounted to him by persons involved.

Background material on immigration is from *Historical Statistics of the United States, Colonial Times to 1957*. Oscar Handlin, in *The Newcomers* (New York, 1962), has much useful information.

Shrinkage of unskilled work in total American production is described in *Manpower Report of The President*, March, 1963, and *Historical Statistics*.

Housing statistics are from *Statistical Abstract of the United States*, 1962.

The description of changes in the American city and their impact on impoverished residents was much aided by "The Social Implications of Urban Redevelopment," by Peter Marris, in the *American Institute of Planners Journal*, August, 1962.

CHAPTER THREE (pages 29–41)

Description of family circumstances is based on interviews in Uptown Chicago, especially with the man who is called in this account, "Homer Burleigh."

Much useful background on Uptown came from John Donovan and Per Lykke of the Uptown office of the Chicago Youth Commission. Particularly valuable insight came from Victor Streufert of Concordia Teachers College, who in pursuit of his own strong feelings and academic graduate work lived among impoverished white migrants from the South.

CHAPTER FOUR (pages 42–62)

Material about the Johnson family is from personal interviews by the author.

Cultural and economic changes in mountain areas of the East are discussed in *Life and Religion in Southern Appalachia,* Wetherford and Brewer. I am also indebted to Victor Streufert for observations from his studies and personal experiences.

Logan County mining employment data are from officials of the United Mine Workers of America.

Sales tax data are from the U.S. Internal Revenue Service.

Material on diet of the poor is based on *Food, The Yearbook of Agriculture,* 1959, 576-588; "Family Food Plans and Food Costs," Home Economics Research Report, No. 20, Agricultural Research Service, U.S. Department of Agriculture, plus interviews with nutrition analysts in the Department of Agriculture and the National Research Council. Not enough is known about undernourishment in the United States. One reason is that it, like poverty, has receded just enough to remove the massive, classic evidence, like pellagra, beriberi and rickets. But like poverty it remains in significant forms in modern demands for

intellectual attentiveness, emotional control, and long attention spans, lack of which can hamper the individual in
education and white collar competition as the traditional
vitamin failures crippled him in purely physical competition. Contemporary deficiencies also show up in secondary
ways through greater incidence of pneumonia, tuberculosis,
and early death, and this, too, calls for a different and more
subtle measurement.

Federal studies are done chiefly by the Department of
Agriculture which tends to measure quantities of food dis-
pensed and purchased, rather than the pathology of poor
food among large populations. The Public Health Service
which might ordinarily study the incidence of food-related
disease is pre-empted from this field by Agriculture's traditional dominance. Furthermore, all surveys of undernourishment in the United States are inadequate compared to
some other highly developed industrial countries. The basic
survey in this country is done every ten years. A similar
study is done in England, for example, every year. Useful
work is done by individual states and some local departments of social welfare which need such information, but
they cannot do the country-wide and broad population
sampling that is needed to give the data national validity.

The effect of the Federal Food Stamp program on
welfare recipients in West Virginia is from Mrs. Grace
Strain, Supervisor, Food Stamp Program, West Virginia
Department of Welfare, and from a copy of the original
letter of W. P. Phipps.

CHAPTER FIVE (pages 63–77)

Material for this chapter includes observations from periods spent in the West Madison area Skid Row in Chicago and in San Francisco's Skid Row.

Population size, disease and death rates on Skid Row came from "The Homeless Man on Skid Row," a study prepared for the Tenants Relocation Bureau of the City of Chicago by the National Opinion Research Center.

Captain Stanley Davey of the Salvation Army Harbor Light, San Francisco, provided background observations on lives of some men the author interviewed. An unusually perceptive description of poverty and of Skid Row life came from the man referred to in this chapter as "Paul," who had been poor and alcoholic for many years but had returned to previous disciplines in scholarly work and is writing a master's thesis. The San Francisco Redevelopment Agency provided useful guidance.

CHAPTER SIX (pages 78–91)

Material on the man referred to as "John Merrick" came from personal interviews by the author.

Background data came from James N. Williams, Urban League of Rhode Island.

CHAPTER SEVEN (pages 92–102)

Material on Columbus Cooper is from personal interviews by the author plus the records and assistance of L. S. James, field representative of the South Carolina Council on Human Relations and of the National Sharecroppers Fund.

Material on reduction of farm manpower and distribution of farm income is from Edward Higbee, *New York Times Magazine*, June 2, 1963; "Hired Farm Workers in the United States," June, 1961, U.S. Department of Labor; and from interviews with officials of the Domestic Activities of the Farm Placement Service of the U.S. Department of Labor.

The status of Negro farmers is from "A Better Life for Farm Families," National Sharecroppers Fund; and "A Study of Negro Farmers in South Carolina," Southern Regional Council.

CHAPTER EIGHT (pages 103–111)

Material on the man referred to as "Edmund Mac-Intosh" is based on personal interviews by the author.

Data on the aged are from "New Population Facts on Older Americans, 1960," a Staff Report to the Special Committee on Aging, U.S. Senate, 1961.

General background on the concentration of the aged around Bunker Hill came from Miss Margaret Watkins and Jaime Monroy, of the Community Redevelopment Agency, Los Angeles.

CHAPTER NINE (pages 112–123)

Material on living conditions is based on interviews with migrant workers in camps along Route 441, Florida and with the Reverend and Mrs. William Bell of the Migrant Missionary Fellowship, Pompano Beach, Florida. Statistical material is from *Migratory Labor*, hearings before the Subcommittee on Migratory Labor, U.S. Senate, Volumes I and II, 1959; "Hired Farm Workers in the United States," June, 1961, U.S. Department of Labor, B.E.S. No. R-200; and interviews with officials of the Farm Placement Service of the U.S. Department of Labor, and with Robert Cooney, of the AFL-CIO.

Material on the mechanization of harvesting and field work is from, "Impact of Technological Advances in Agriculture, Summary of State Reports," U.S. Department of Labor, May, 1961.

CHAPTER TEN (pages 124–140)

Material about personal circumstances of Papago Indians is from personal interviews in the Papago Indian Reservation. Much useful information came from Eugene Johnson, chairman of the tribal council, and the local superintendent of the Bureau of Indian Affairs, Thomas St. Clair, and his staff. Background data are from "The Papago Development Program," Bureau of Indian Affairs, May, 1949; the *Annals* of the American Academy of Political and Social Science, May, 1957; "Papago Reservation Report, 1962," The Arizona Commission on Indian Affairs; "An Outline of Papago Culture," U.S. Public Health Service, Phoenix; a letter May 16, 1963 from Mrs. Jean Nowak, Chief of Information Services, Division of Indian Health, U.S. Public Health Service; and personal interviews with Professor William Kelly, Director of the Bureau of Ethnic Research of the University of Arizona; Brother Stanley of St. Catherine's Mission, Topawa; and Dr. S. C. Binder, superintendent of the U.S. Public Health Service Hospital in Sells, Arizona.

CHAPTER ELEVEN (pages 141–160)

Description of family circumstances is based on interviews with families living on Chicago's West Side in the West Adams Street-Jackson Boulevard area.

Quoted material from Sister Mary William and Gordon Austin is from personal interviews and observations.

CHAPTER TWELVE (pages 161–171)

The first paragraph is from *Strangers and Neighbors*, published in 1952 by the Anti-Defamation League, New York.

The second paragraph is from *The Welsh in America: Letters from the Immigrants*, edited by Alan Conway, University of Minnesota Press, Minneapolis. Copyright 1961 by the University of Minnesota.

The blurring of role of father and mother within the family is reflected in Department of Labor data showing a doubling in the number of married women working in the last fifteen years. The National Industrial Conference Board (*New York Times*, May 29, 1963) said that by 1960 one-third of all married women held jobs. This hits low-income families with disproportionate psychological effect because in such families the mother's working is often an obvious necessity because of the father's unemployment or underemployment. If the father is idle, the absence of the wife at work makes the household reversal unmistakable.

The legal questions in surveillance of welfare recipients are discussed in "Poverty and the Law," a mimeographed memorandum published March 25, 1963 by the National Social Welfare Assembly, New York.

The study of closed aid-to-dependent–children welfare cases is in *An American Dependency Challenge*, by M. Elaine Burgess and Daniel O. Price of the Institute for Research in Social Sciences of the University of North Carolina and published by the American Public Welfare Association, Chicago.

CHAPTER THIRTEEN (pages 172–193)

There were 181 deaths from pleurisy in the United States in 1962, according to the U.S. Public Health Service, or a rate of one in one million.

Average family income for 1960 is from Table 443, *Statistical Abstract, 1962,* and is a composite of family and unrelated individual personal incomes, including non-cash benefits. It is a simple mathematical average. Figures on percentages of families and individuals on various levels of income is from Table 444 of the *Abstract;* it, too, includes non-cash income.

Statistics on "modest but adequate" budgets are from the Office of Business Economics and the U.S. Department of Labor and are graphed with unusual clarity in *Poverty and Deprivation in the United States,* published by the Conference on Economic Progress, 1962.

The level of income needed for adequate medical care is discussed in "Medical Indigence," Division Report Series No. 11, Research Department, Health and Welfare Council, Inc., Philadelphia, though the report does not give data on actual expenditures on health. A 6 per cent figure was assumed for medical and dental care in the family budget, a rough average from the series of studies "Consumer Expenditures and Income, 1960-61," by the Bureau of Labor Statistics.

The number of men, women, and children who are poor was derived from data in the "Current Population Reports, Consumer Income," Bureau of the Census, Series P-60, No. 39, February 28, 1963. The totals for varying levels of income are from the same source.

There is a bothersome discrepancy between the income figures from the Office of Business Economics (OBE) and Department of Labor and those from the Bureau of the Census. The OBE obtains its information mainly from income tax reports checked by surveys and includes in its data non-cash income such as food and fuel produced and consumed on farms and the net rental value of owner-occupied homes. The figures from the Bureau of the Census are more detailed, are obtained from surveys of 25,000 representative households in 638 counties, but include only cash income. The overall discrepancy between counting cash incomes and incomes with both cash and non-cash equivalents is five per cent, though not distributed evenly among all income levels. Thus, the requirements for a "modest" income include non-cash benefits but the figures of total numbers in poverty do not. I used the cash-plus-non-cash data on family budgets because they are the most comprehensive available, but unfortunately they are not broken down below $2,000 levels and there are other gaps precisely at the levels of poverty.

The Census data are most detailed for what families receive; they are broken down to $500 stages and are more particular for specific family sizes. But these reflect cash income only. This discrepancy leaves the two sides of the poverty equation as presented here slightly out of joint but not, I think, intolerably. For one thing, the non-cash benefits of food, fuel and rent are concentrated on farm families which constitute 17 per cent of the poor; the vast majority of the people described as poor in this book are not affected in a substantial way. (There are some 1961 data in these calculations, combined with 1960, and this adds a negligible discrepancy. The all-family average increase in income between 1960 and 1961 was $120. Almost certainly the increase was even less among the poor because their incomes generally are among the most sluggish in the economy, with small farm income relatively insensitive and welfare budgets and marginal jobs among the last to adjust to increases in cost of living and changes in the value of the dollar.)

Lastly, deciding what level of income constitutes poverty necessarily involves personal judgment. There is almost no national information on what a family needs in dollars for minimal food, shelter and health. There are local welfare estimates but these reflect local costs and local standards which differ drastically from place to place. There are vague rules-of-thumb on what percentages of a "modest" income is an "emergency" budget, but these are not based on any good scientific nationwide data on modern nutritional intake by such families, nor the social and pathological effect of poor housing and health care. Inevitably, there is guesswork and a certain amount of instinct involved where the scientific information is missing. I was influenced by families I saw living on known cash incomes, which I could usually determine with some reliability through welfare sources and other records. It is interesting, therefore, that I chose $3,000 as the family *cash* income level as the definition of poverty, deliberately low because of the guesswork involved and because non-cash income was not taken into account, and using the Census figures for numbers of people living under strictly cash incomes, I obtained a total of 36,000,000 poor. The Conference on Economic Progress, using $4,000 as the definition of family poverty, higher because it did include both cash and non-cash benefits for a family, and using the less detailed (but still useful above the $2000-level) OBE data that described the number of people living at given levels of cash *and non-cash* income, obtained a total of 38,000,000 poor.

Characteristics of the poor, statistically, are from *Poverty and Deprivation in the United States,* published by the Conference on Economic Progress.

Status of the Negro is from "The Economic Situation of Negroes in the United States," Bulletin S-3, Revised 1962, U.S. Department of Labor.

Educational characteristics are from "Income of Families and Persons in the United States, 1961," *Current Population Reports,* Table 8. Median school years of heads of families with less than $3,000 annual income ranges from 8.4 to 8.8. Of heads of families in that income bracket, 46.4 per cent had less than eight years of schooling.

The study of the Packard Motor Company closing was done by Harold L. Sheppard, Louis A. Ferman and Seymour Faber, of Wayne State University, for the Special Committee on Unemployment Problems of the U.S. Senate. Of a sample of men who had been returned to work,

22 per cent were in jobs in a firm associated with Packard and had gone there by direct company reference; 58 per cent found jobs through friends and neighbors; 14 per cent through want ads, employment agencies, and personal applications; and 6 per cent "other." Eliminating those placed in the Packard-associated company, 75 per cent were re-employed through some intercession of friends and neighbors.